D0619930

BEST OF STORE DESIGN

Imprint
The Deutsche Bibliothek is registering this publication in the Deutsche Nationalbibliographie; detailed bibliographical information can be found on the internet at http://dnb.ddb.de

ISBN 978-3-03768-024-7

www.braun-publishing.ch

1st edition 2009

Project coordinator: Annika Schulz
Editorial staff: Nadja Mahler
Translation: Stephen Roche, Hamburg
Graphic concept: Michaela Prinz

BEST OF STORE DESIGN

BRAUN

Preface

Dagmar Glück

A shoe is an item of footwear with a firm sole, whose primary purpose is to protect the foot. But a shoe is also much more than that. The purchase of a pair of shoes represents – especially for women – a highly emotional moment. And rarely does it end with the shoes. The shoes, after all, require a handbag and a perfectly fitting dress to match, not to mention novel earrings and that stunning top... and already the lady has succumbed to shopping fever. While this scenario may be a well-worn cliché, shopping is certainly much more than simply the exchange of money for goods.

Shopping is celebrated as a sensual, even passionate, experience that also promotes our sense of taste. The retail industry is ever-changing, and the range of goods on offer in the marketplace is enormous. That is why the ambience of the store is decisive in determining where we spend our money. It is the job of architects and interior designers to create the basis for this ambience. Shop! Best of Store Design looks at the success stories of contemporary merchandise presentation and takes the reader on a shopping spree through 47 of the hottest shops in the world's hippest cities. The spectrum of retail design extends from flashy designer stores to high-class boutiques and the grand flagship stores of major brands. Whether in New York, Paris or Tokyo, Buenos Aires or Berlin, modern stores express the zeitgeist of consumption. They require creative ideas and individual solutions. Every one of the designs featured in this book is unique and tailored to the needs of the respective store.

In a situation where every trend comes hot on the heels of the next, interior design at point of sale needs to be sustainable and

AIR PRESTO
WAFFLE RACER II
AIR 180
Through runners had been enjoying the benefits of Nike Air since its 1978 debut in the Tailwind, it was nearly a decade before anyone besides product developers or factory workers got a glimpse of the Air-Sole unit behind the technology. Once Visible Air debuted in 1987, the next evolution would be only a few years in the making. Launched in 1991 with a campaign featuring a series of works by international artists, the Air 180 sported an Air-Sole unit that was not only 50% larger than any before it, but featured 180° visibility around the bottom of the outsole—hence the Air 180 name.

flexible, and must precisely meet the requirements of a new fashion collection. That is why we find minimalist design with reduced color schemes and forms next to hip and imaginative shopping realms. Whether the store sells shoes, jewelry and clothing, or cell phones and laptops, the goal is the same: to create the perfect showcase for the particular merchandise and the target clientele. While variety is the spice of life, and even more so of the retail trade, the customer is also king. Ultimately the store design must appeal to him/her.

Shopping is in a state of flux. We can now purchase almost any product through the Internet and have it conveniently delivered to our homes. The traditional retail store can only prevail against this competition if it succeeds in creating an added value that could never come through the Internet: Sensuality. Only in real-life shops can customers touch the merchandise, try it out or on, and ideally carry it in their arms to the cashier's desk. A store thrives when its customers are wowed by the shopping experience, and spread the word about their favorite place to shop. That's why retailers are investing increasingly in architectural quality as a central element of their sales strategy. Through a finely tuned use of light and color, exclusive materials and eccentric forms, every retailer has the chance to rise above the competition. The La Phil Bookstore in Los Angeles is an example of this idea in action. It is unlike any other bookstore: in place of packed shelves and overflowing presentation tables, the bookworms of the future will find here a graceful structure with narrow timber battens that resemble the pages of a book. The furniture, which was designed by Belzberg Architects, offers the ideal presentation space for erudite goods.

The store itself and the products on display are equally effective marketing instruments as television advertising or sponsoring. This insight is new yet promises great opportunity. For architects it lays down the challenge of contributing to brand identity through design. In New York's Fifth Avenue the stores of the top fashion labels stand next to one another. It is no easy task to make a store stand out on this street. Armani has succeeded thanks to an unusual and eye-catching feature: a stairway designed by Doriana & Massimiliano Fuksas whose striking form reverberates throughout the store. At the same time this architectural feature fulfils the practical function of taking customers to the upper floor.

Routes such as this through the store represent not only effective merchandise presentation and optimal space usage, but are also key design elements. The more products a customer views, the more s/he will buy. If the design succeeds in enticing customers to the furthest corners of the store, this will be reflected in the store's sales turnover. However, the customer should never sense this sober calculation. The customer is king, and his kingdom is the designed space, the shopping paradise. In this realm goods become fetishes. In Kymyka, a store in the Dutch city of Maastricht, customers sense an appropriately mystical ambience. Maurice Mentjen's design is reminiscent of the Garden of Eden. It's most charming features are the lightness of the design and the tension between yin and yang. The shoes are presented in an almost weightless fashion on filigree steel stilts. The women's department is decorated in virginal white, while men's fashions are presented against a black backdrop. This design concept is both striking and memorable.

The tension between the male and the female is also represented in the behavior of shoppers. That shopping is primarily a woman's pastime is not merely a cliché. While men tend to hone in on what they want to buy and leave the store as quickly as possible, statistics show that women spend considerably more time shopping. No other factor exerts a greater influence on the extent of the purchase than the amount of time people spend in a store. When couples shop together, impatient men, by their very presence, impinge on valuable sales. One solution for the obstacle men present to shopping is to provide comfortable seating. Another is the A1Store in Vienna. Power, coolness and precision – BEHF Ebner Hasenauer Ferenczy have translate the values of the brand into a store design. These and other examples show that successful interior design can awaken passion in even the most stubborn shopping grouch: for the stylish briefcase, the cool wristwatch, the well-fitting shirt and maybe even for a stunning item of footwear.

20 Peacocks | New York | L.E.FT Architects

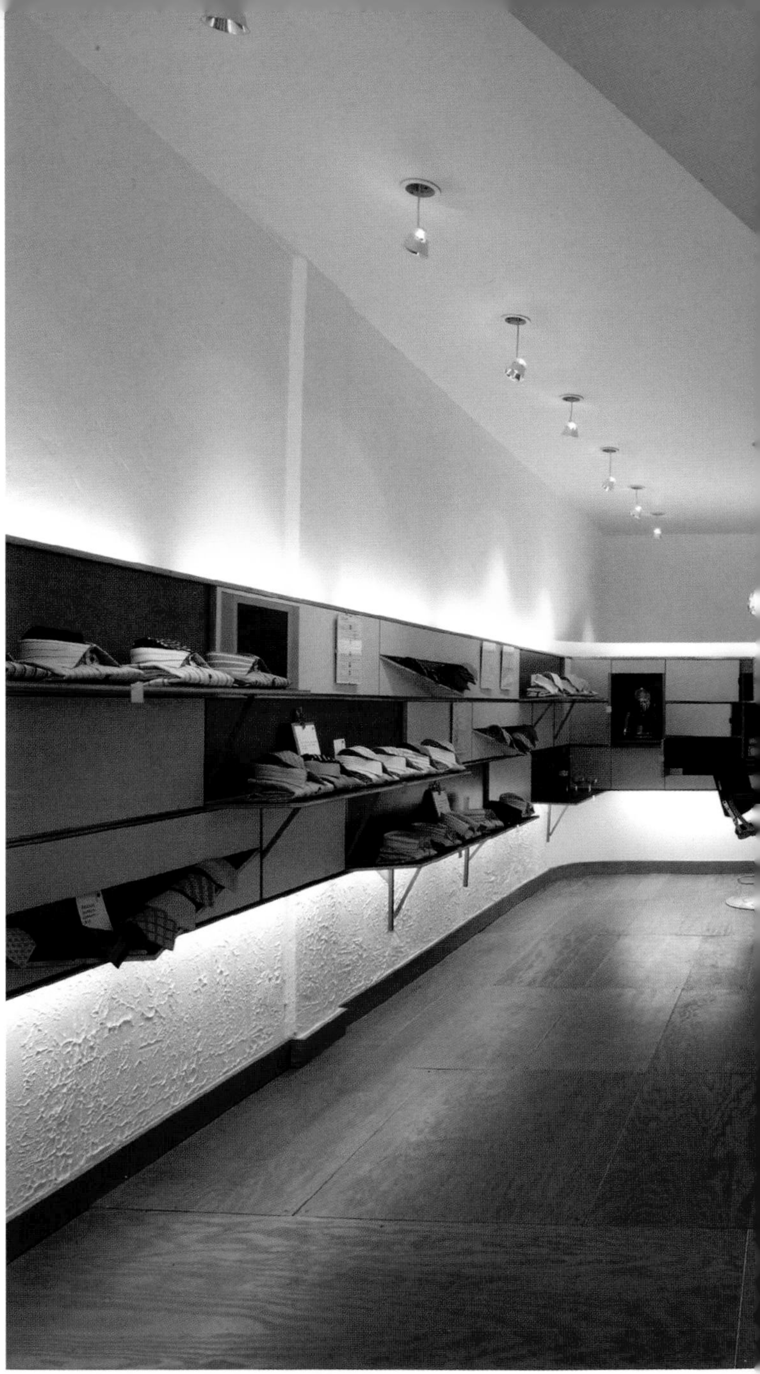

The store is transformed into an articulation that uses the torso as its design guideline

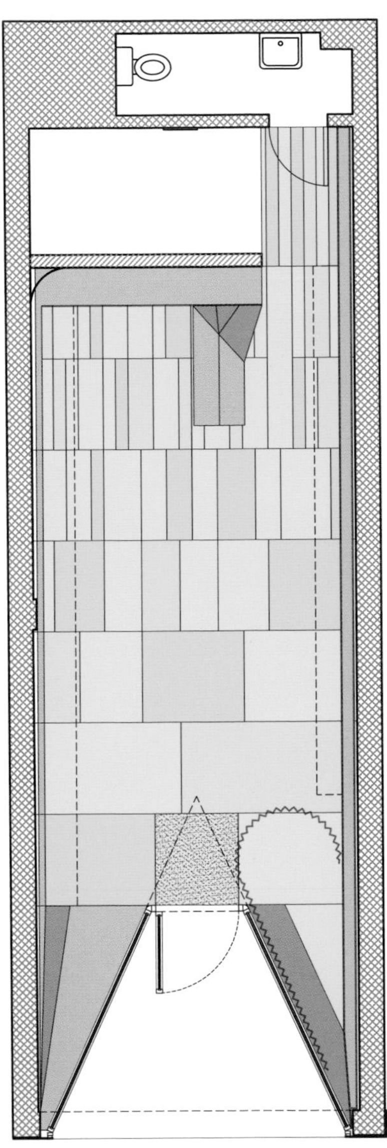

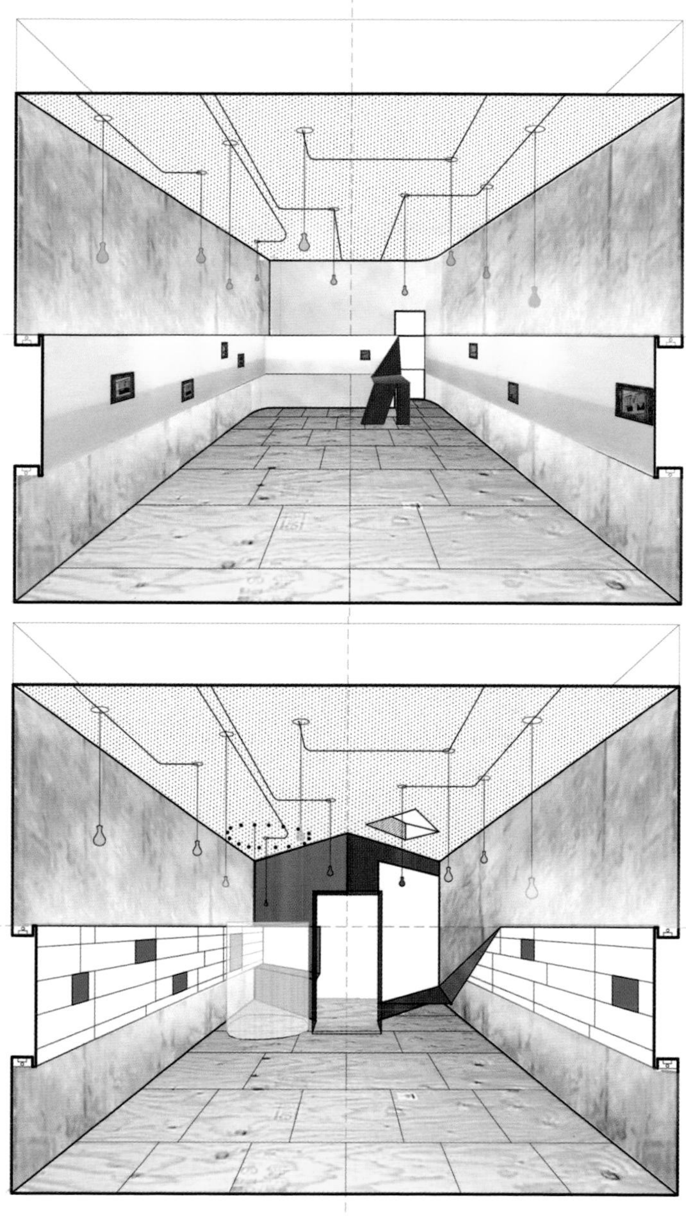

The store is **being developed** into a **three** dimensional box with the **aim of creating** a **unique spatial** experience

A1

A1

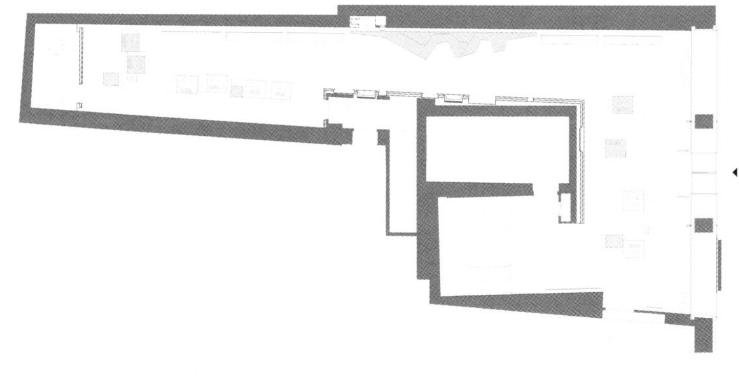
0 1 2 5

A1

HANDYS & TARIFE
• Kristallklar im besten Netz telefonieren
• Top Handys
• Die besten Tarife

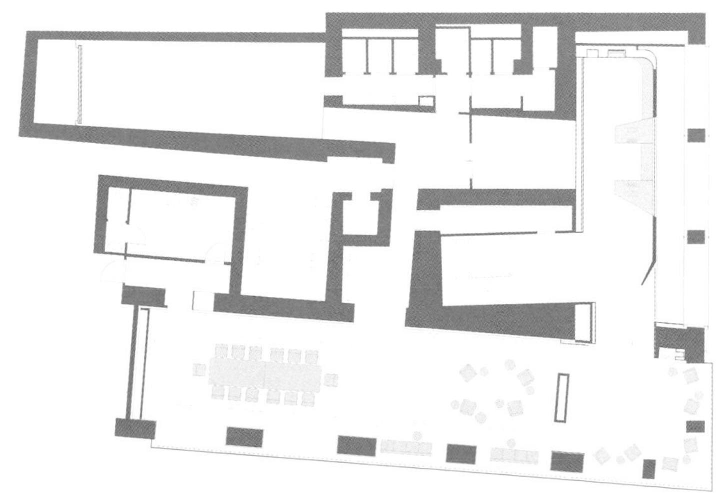

Furniture with **surfaces** of polished **red varnish** and dark leather **contrast with** a curved wall in **maplewood veneer**

A-K-R-I-S-
A-K-R-I-S-
2004

AKRIS
punto

Employing a language of
lightness and
transparency

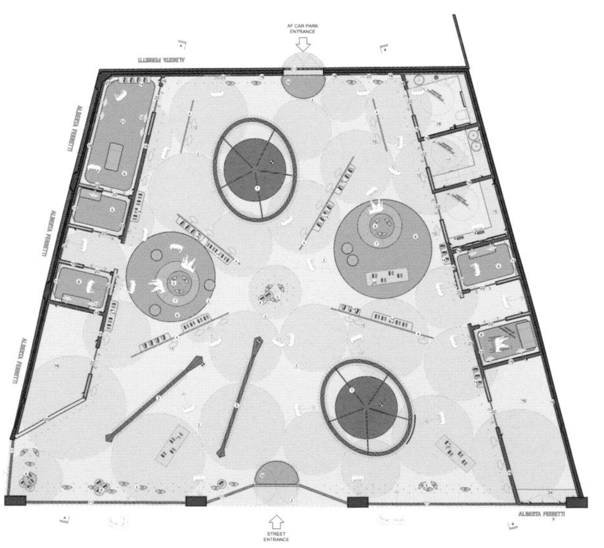
AF CAR PARK
ENTRANCE
ALBERTA FERRETTI
STREET
ENTRANCE

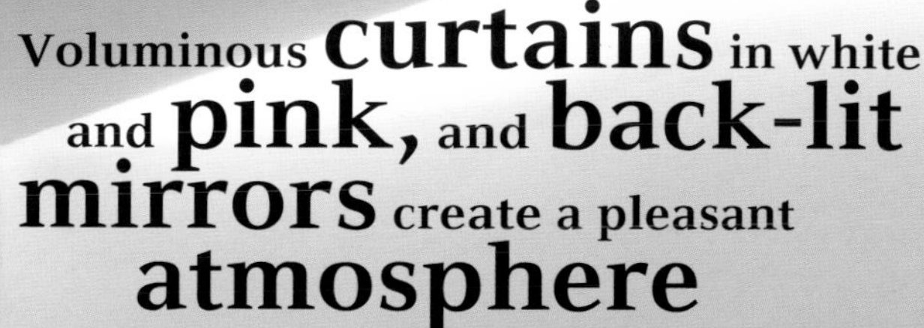

Voluminous **curtains** in white and **pink**, and **back-lit mirrors** create a pleasant **atmosphere**

ALESSA
DESSOUS

The interior design uses
plaster and sheet
aluminum to create
the illusion of
shapes carved from rock

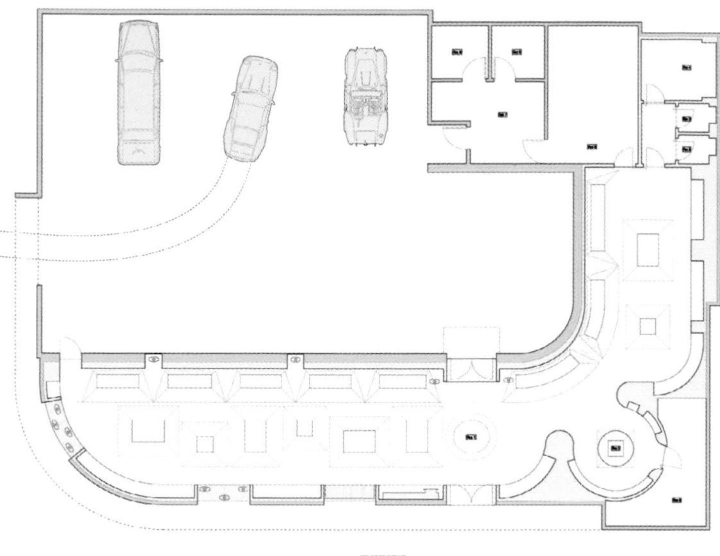
MELROSE AVENUE

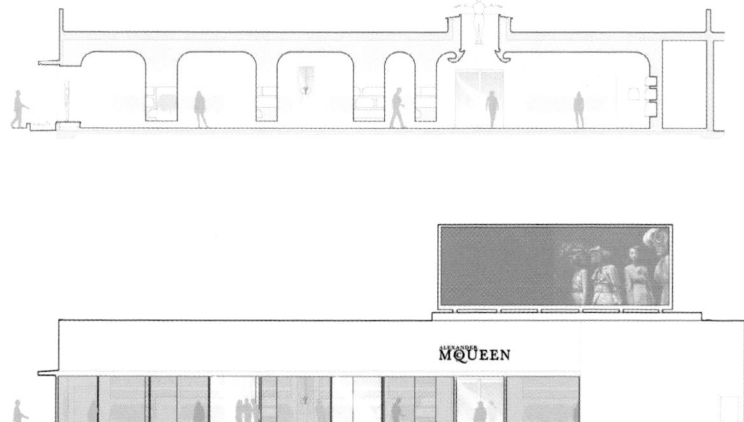
ALEXANDER
MCQUEEN

The design generates territories of activity which are in a state of endless transformation

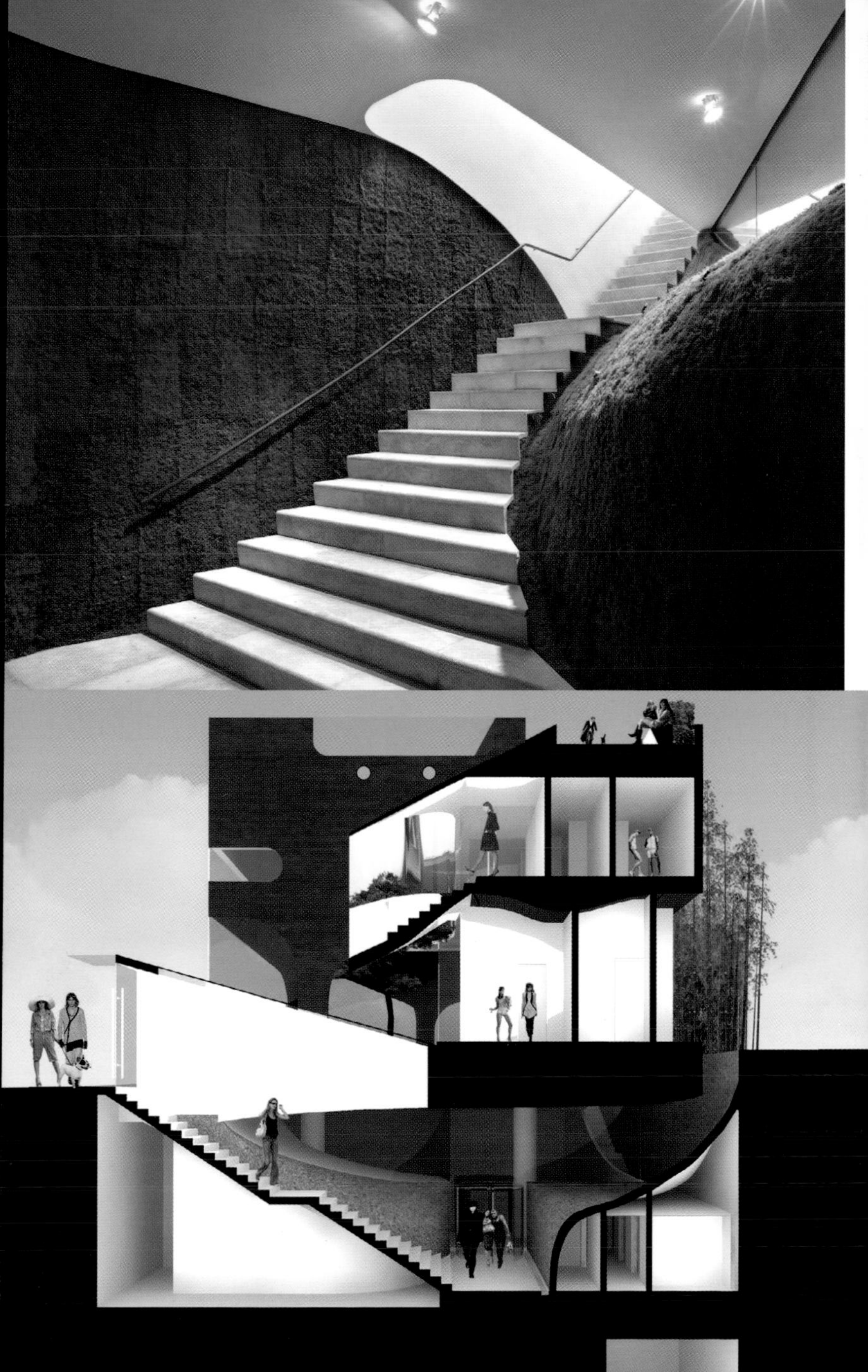

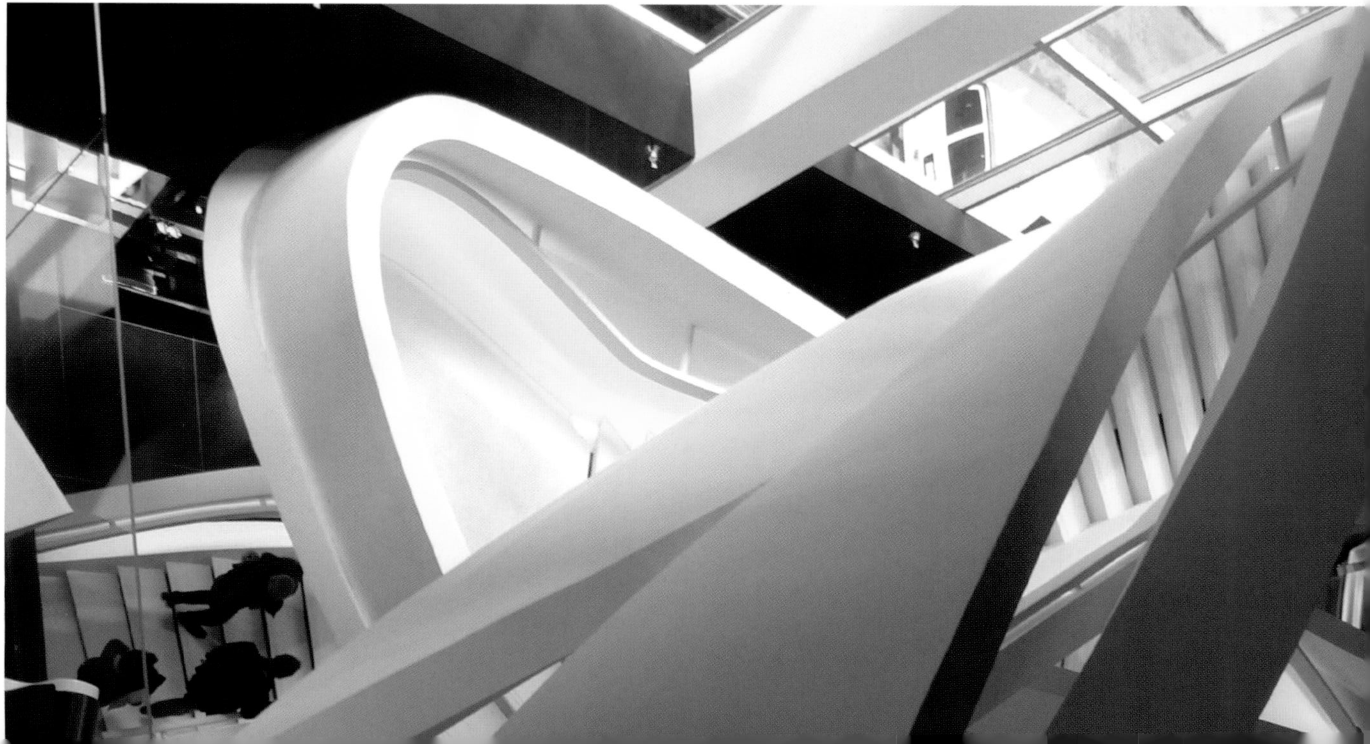

The **nucleus** of the project is the **staircase** that **connects** the floors

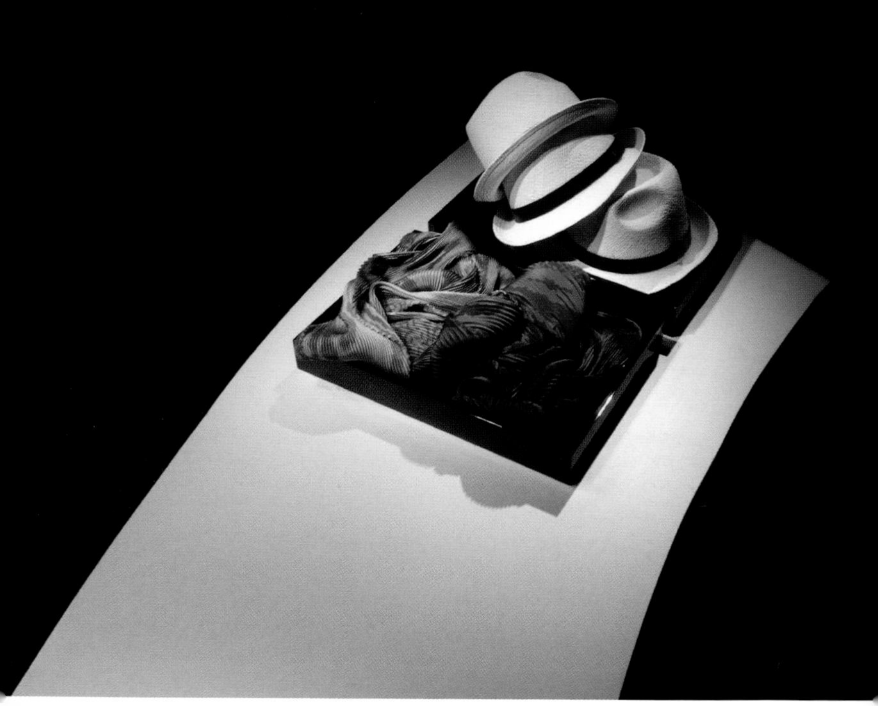

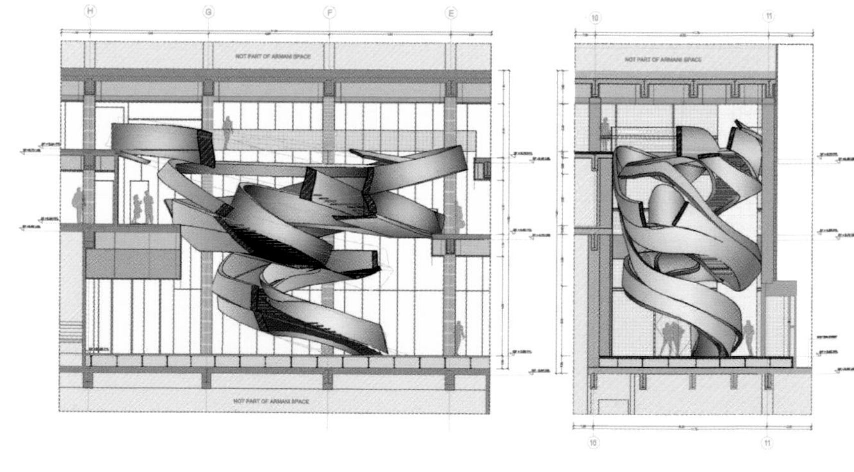
H
G
F
E
NOT PART OF ARMANI SPACE
NOT PART OF ARMANI SPACE
10
11
NOT PART OF ARMANI SPACE
10
11

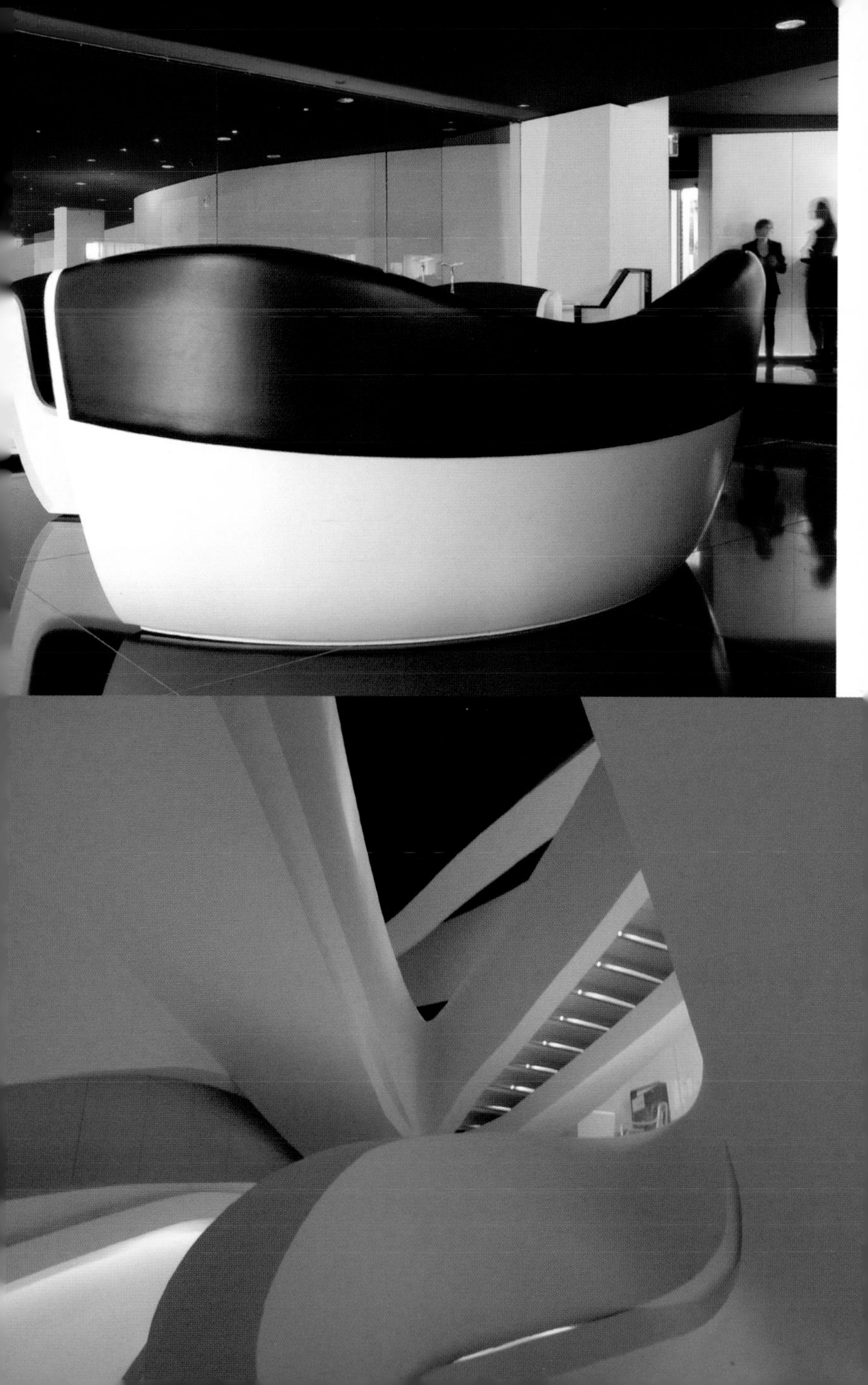

The project seeks to
reproduce in an interior the
feelings and sensations
generated by urban space

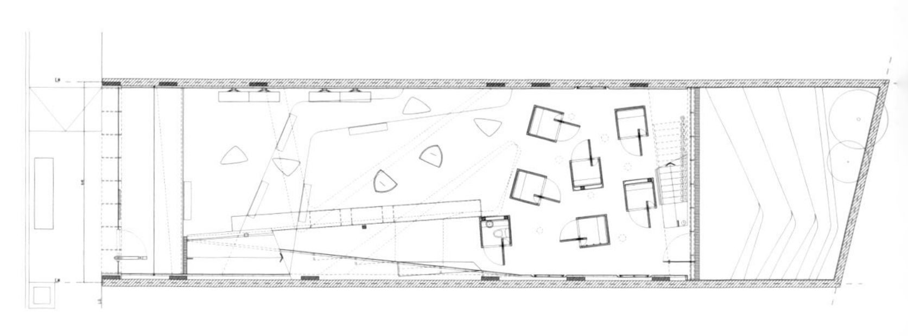

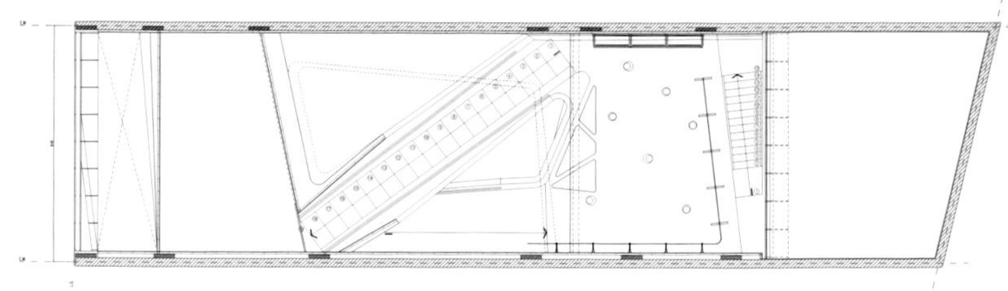

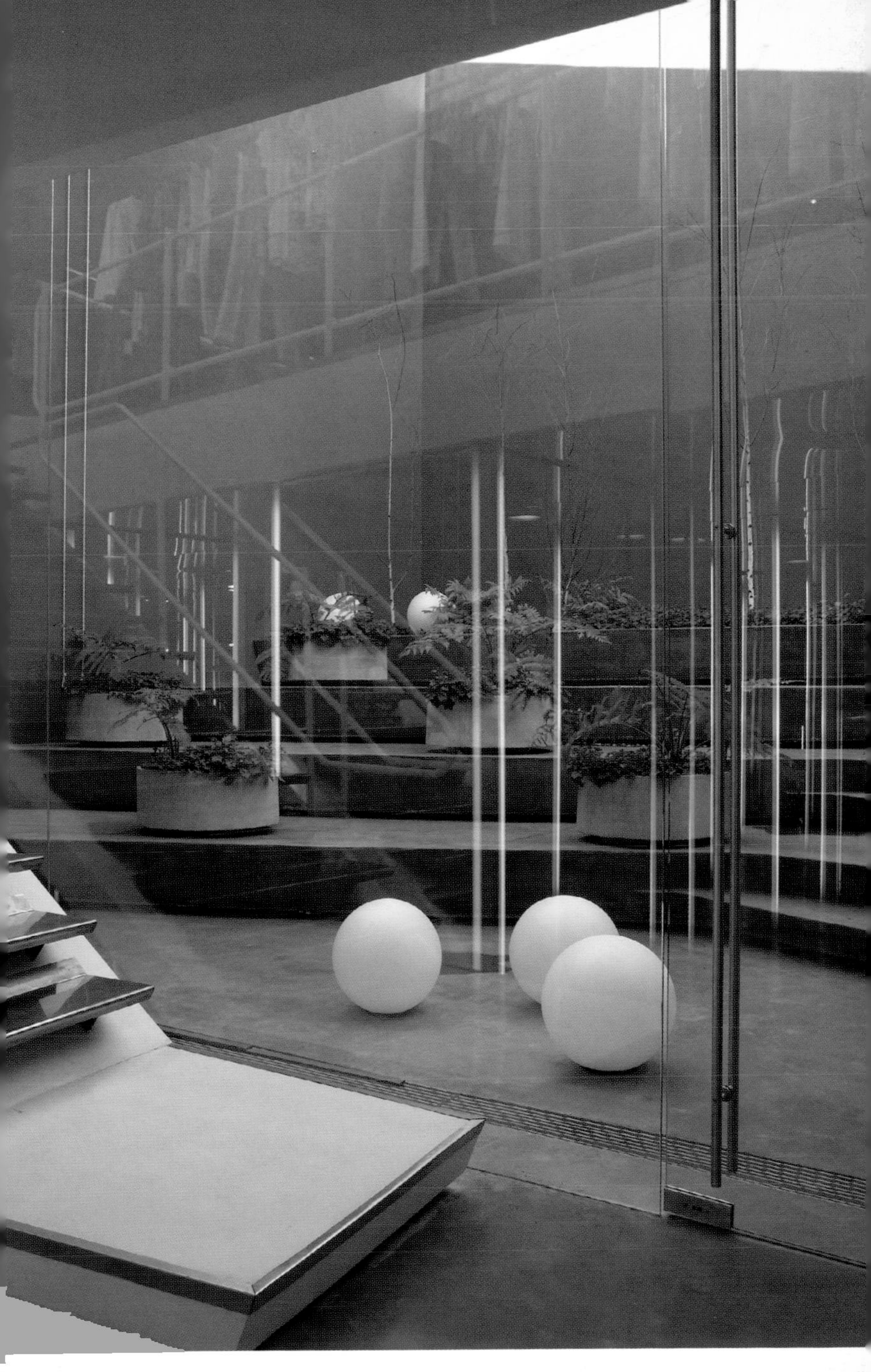

The shop has both a museum-like and an entertaining feel

E SHALL NEV ER

The delicate **transparency** of **lace meets** the robustness of **wool;** brocade meets **organza;** translucent meets **opaque**

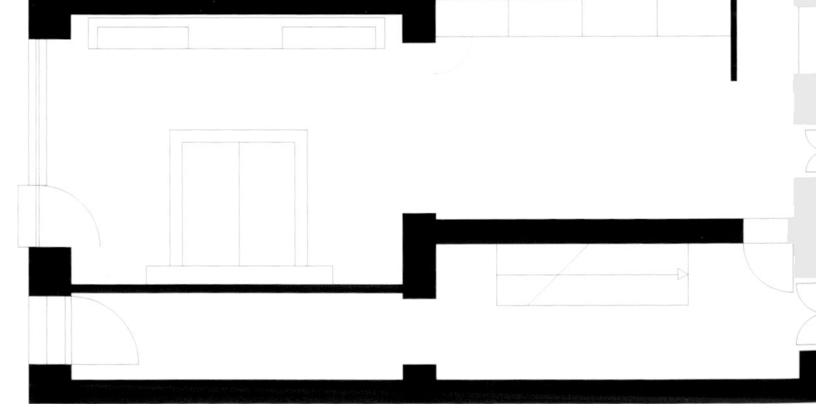

The designers **have created** a seamlessly **fluid ambience** for pleasurable and **experiential** **shopping** and socializing

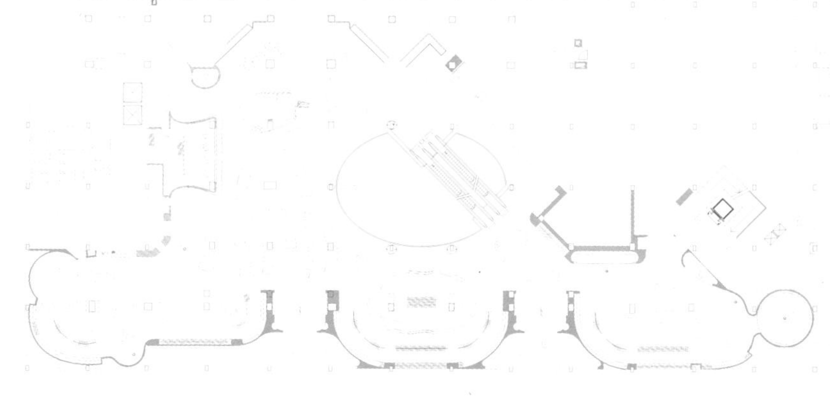

EA7

This shop **is based** on **a concept** of flexibility **and dynamism**

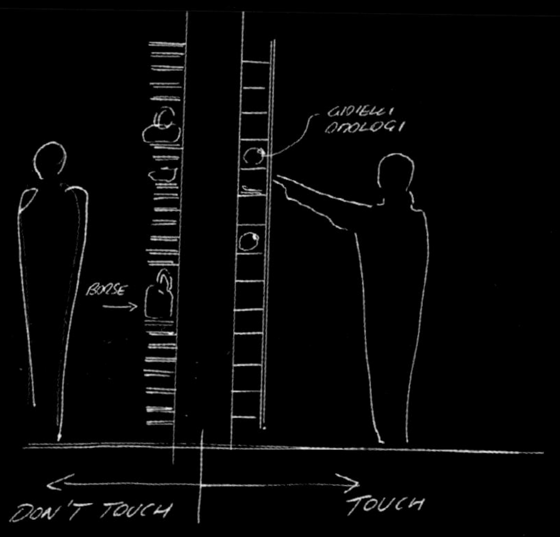
GIOIELLI
OROLOGI
BORSE
DON'T TOUCH
TOUCH

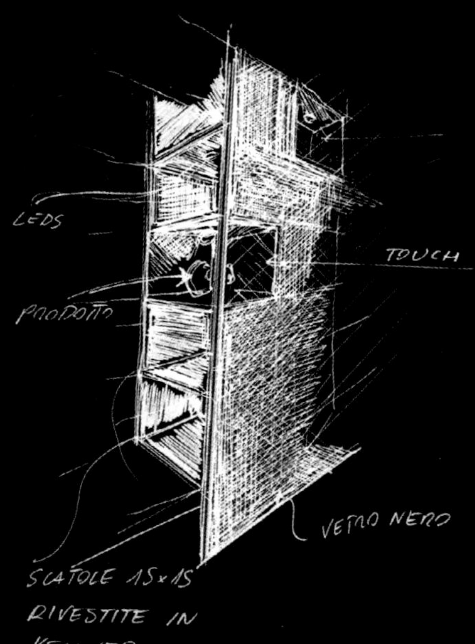
LEDS
TOUCH
PRODOTTO
VETRO NERO
SCATOLE 15×15
RIVESTITE IN
VELLUTO

Identity and diversity **go hand** in hand, generating a **unique personality**

The design embraces rich tones, elaborate textures and a noble form to create a refined backdrop

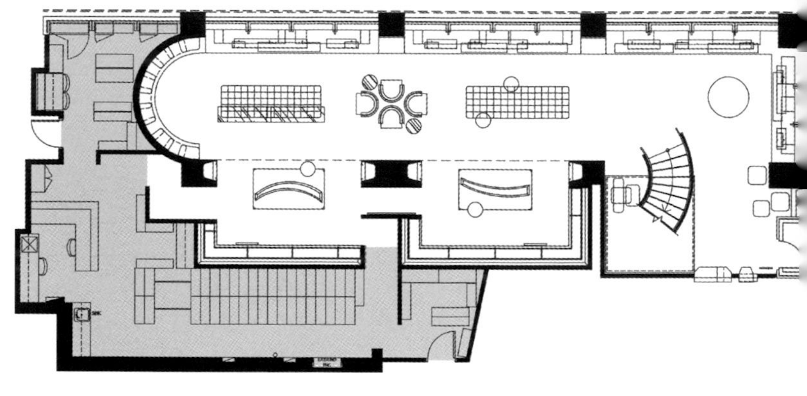

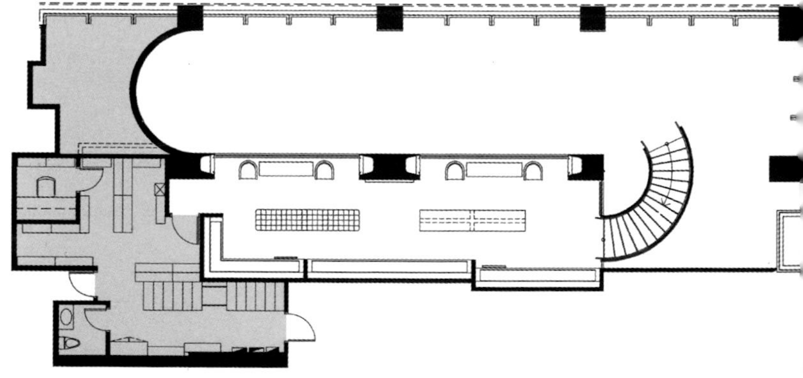

Narrow, vertical glass cases, bordered by **angular columns,** help produce a **gallery-like** atmospher

eko
eko

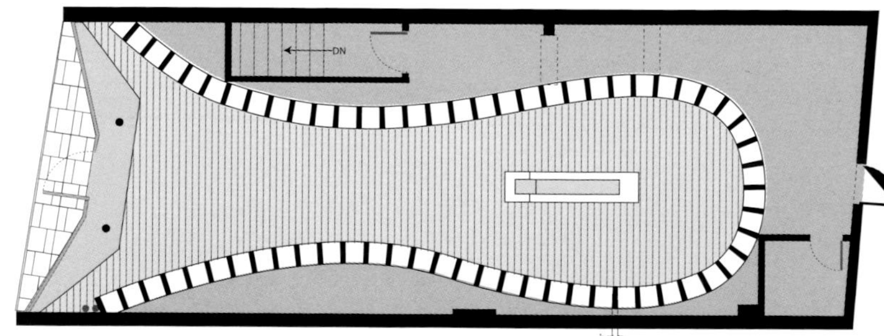
DN

Multi-faceted mirrors
bounce light and
conjure illusions

Basement
tot area=53.28
sqm
Storage
1,88 sqm
FIRE
EXIT
Courtyard
5.40 sqm
-3.33
Toilet
3,00 sqm
-3.33
floor to ceiling
2790mm
main
server
puppet
server
Hi Fi
video
server
audio
contr panel
Vip Room
21.75 sqm
satellite 9
panel 64
kinetic 7
panel 32
satellite 11
panel 18
sub 3
panel 29
floor to ceiling
2810mm
-3.33
satellite 10
panel 93
satellite 12
panel 114
kinetic 8
panel 103
FIRE
EXIT

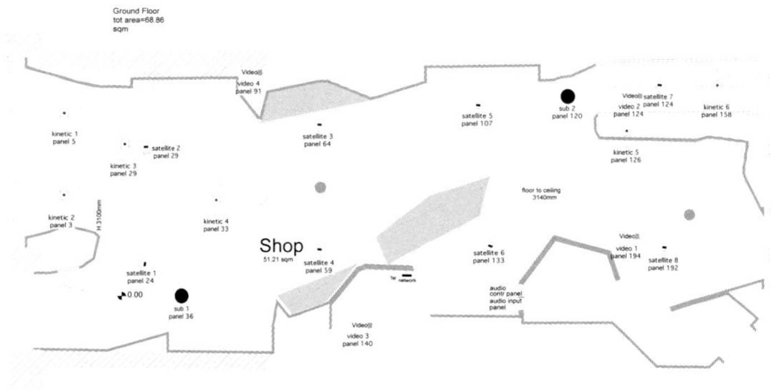

Ground Floor
tot area=68.86
sqm
-3.33
Courtyard
Main access
Video
video 4
panel 91
kinetic 1
panel 5
kinetic 3
panel 29
satellite 2
panel 29
satellite 3
panel 64
satellite 5
panel 107
sub 2
panel 120
Video
video 2
panel 124
satellite 7
panel 124
kinetic 6
panel 158
kinetic 5
panel 126
kinetic 2
panel 3
H 3100mm
kinetic 4
panel 33
floor to ceiling
3140mm
Shop
51.21 sqm
satellite 4
panel 59
satellite 1
panel 24
0.00
sub 1
panel 36
network
satellite 6
panel 133
Video
video 1
panel 194
satellite 8
panel 192
audio
contr panel
audio input
panel
Video
video 3
panel 140

This design plays with the themes of compression, overlapping and transparency, as symbols for dynamism and urbanity

BASIC
SEIDENGLATT

FASHION
SEASONAL
FALKE

LUXURY LINE
No 11
SEA ISLAND COTTON
LUXURY LINE
No 11
SEA ISLAND COTTON
LUXURY LINE
No 11

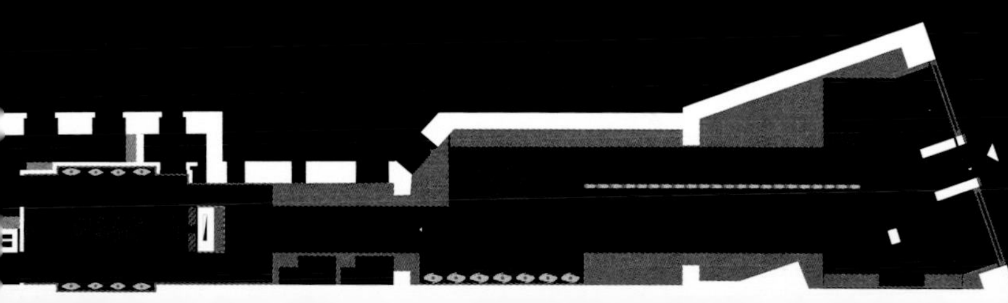

FALKE
MEN
FALKE
WOMEN
FALKE
CHILDREN

Global meets local. The product becomes a theme; the theme a manifes

FREITAG
Top Cat
Dragnet

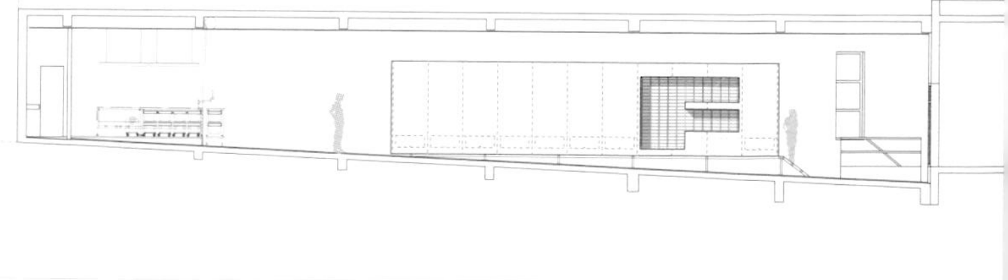

This shop **mixes urban** surfaces, **artistic textures**, concrete and **iron**

White Carrara marble and wax-treated steel highlight the designer's core values of purity and exceptional quality

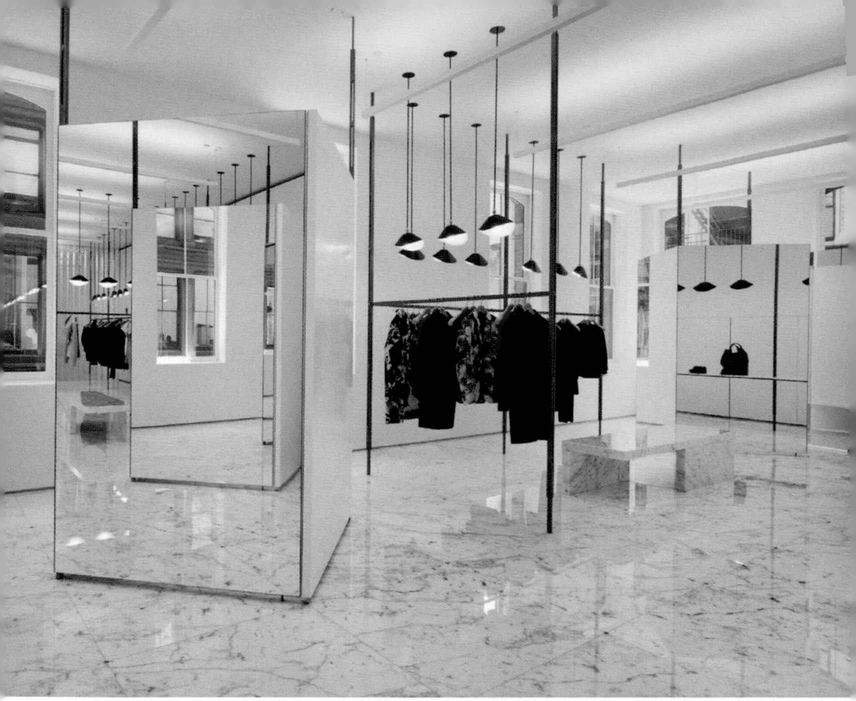

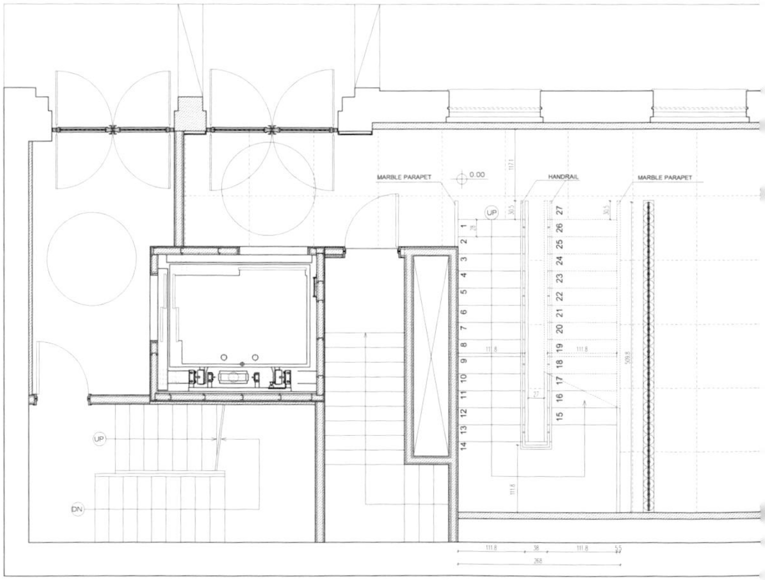

MARBLE PARAPET
0.00
HANDRAIL
MARBLE PARAPET
UP
UP
DN
111.8
38
111.8
5.5
268

This glasses and furnishings store uses wooden furniture as a key design motif

processing
shoes
hat
stock
counter
bag
accessory
glass display
accessory
waiting
examining
purse
belt

Raw and natural materials were used to create an overall industrial feeling

etçii
kuru dinlendirilmiş özel et
dry aged beef

FIRIN

Returning to the origin of fashion, the mother of all the arts

ymyka

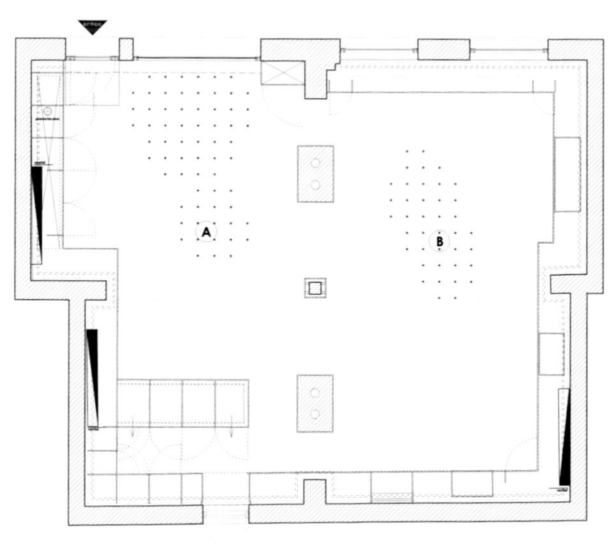
entree
A
B

DSQUARED
DSQUARED

Each individual shel
unit is comprised of a series
of stacked slats

LA PH
INSIDE
DESIGN
NOW
CLASSICAL MUSIC
WOOD

Vitra Design Museum
Miniatures Collection
Vitra Design Museum
Miniatures Collection
FLOWING IN ALL DIRECTIONS

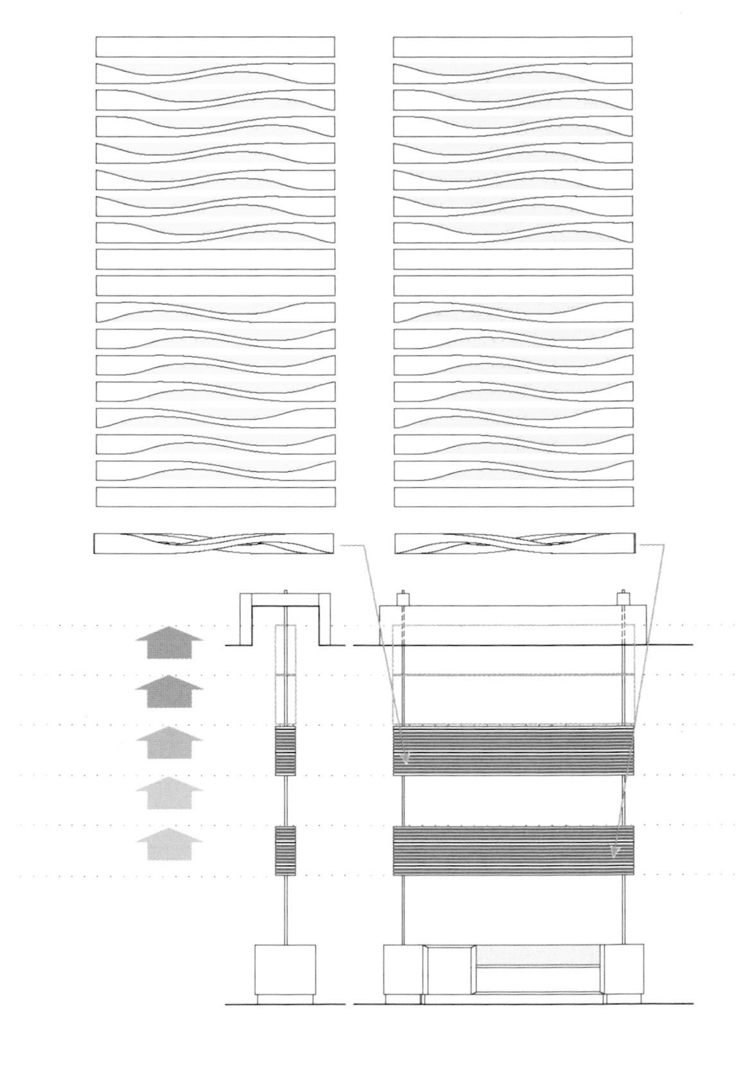

Chopin

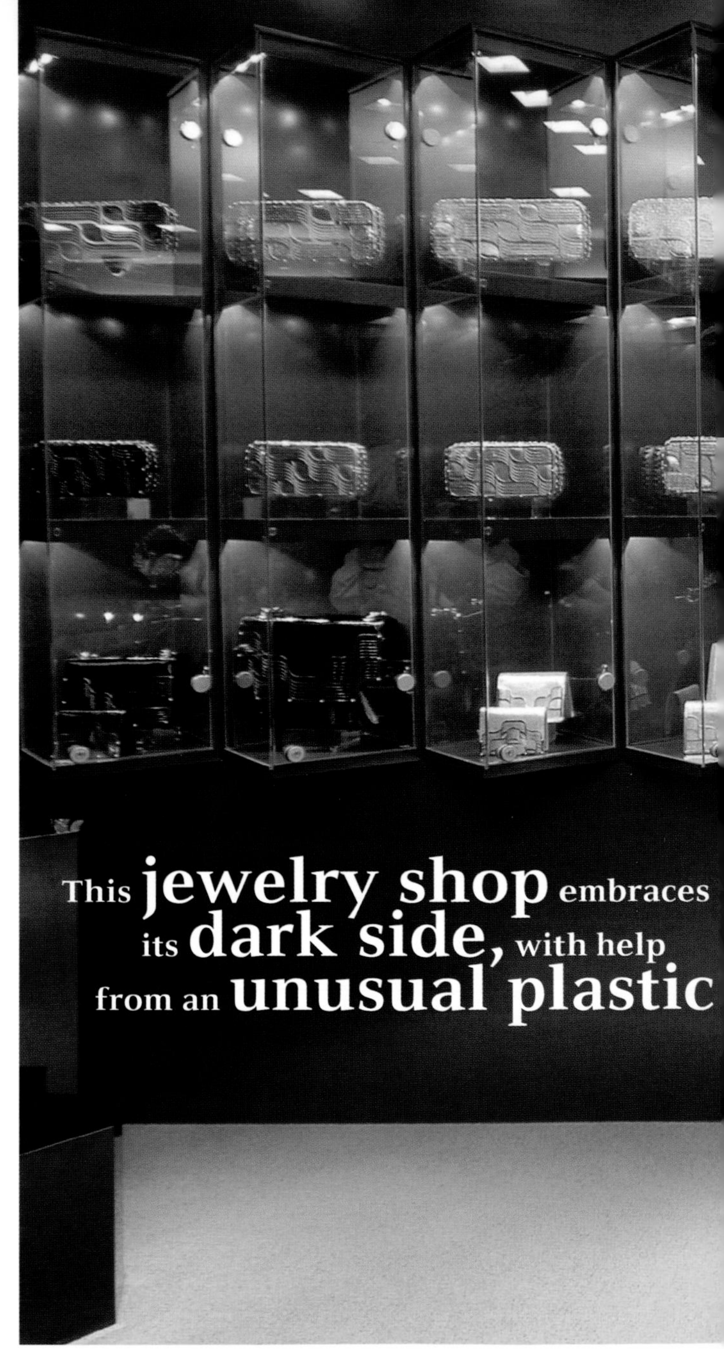

This jewelry shop embraces its dark side, with help from an unusual plastic

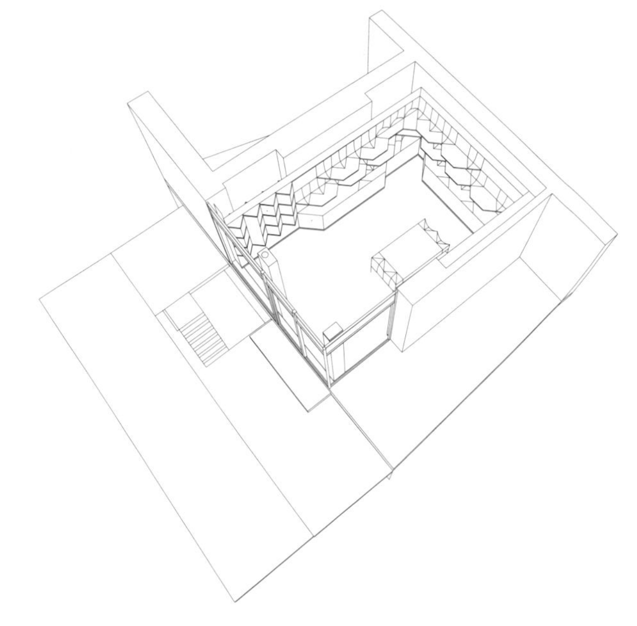

Furniture in various styles and mock musical instruments create an impression of eclectic chic

The space is **defined** by an **industrial concrete** floor and a **series of sharp,** clean **wall** panels

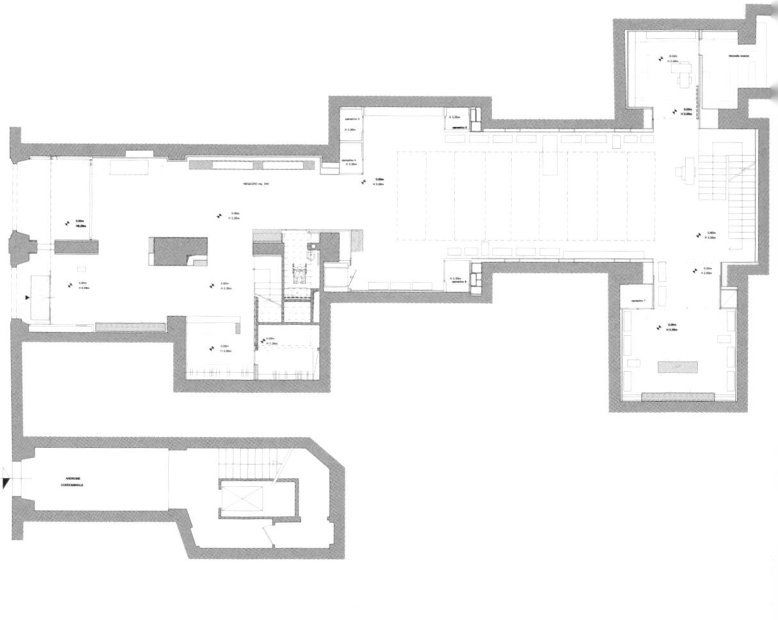

Contrasting **atmospheres** of the conjoined **shops** are unified **by rich** and **diverse material** landscapes

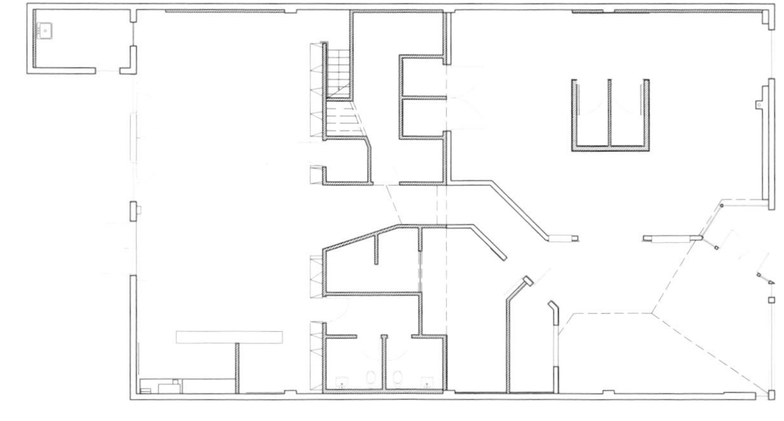

EXIT

EXIT
Garments remodeled by hand

EXIT
0
10

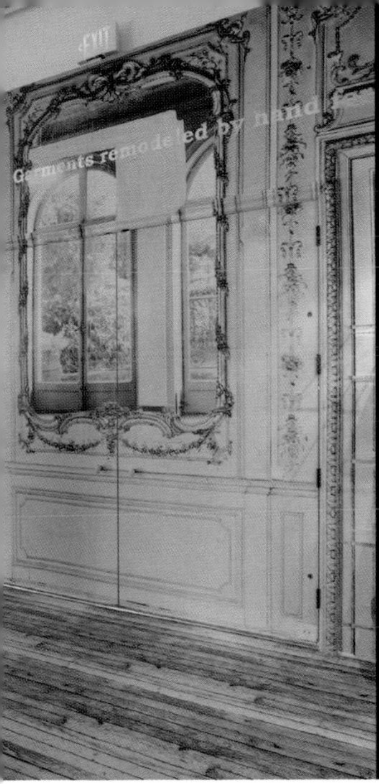

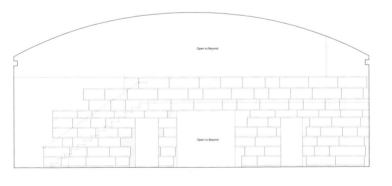

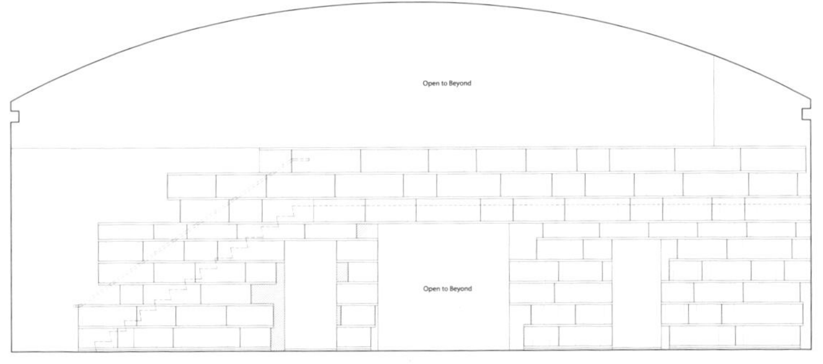

Open to Beyond
Open to Beyond

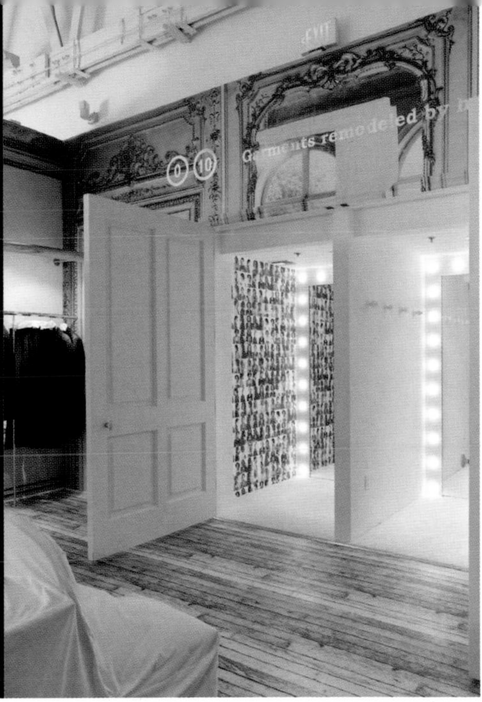

The **architectural** form and the **lighting** are allegories fo
native forests
and **recycling**

Mary's

FURO
SHIKI
FURO
SHIKI

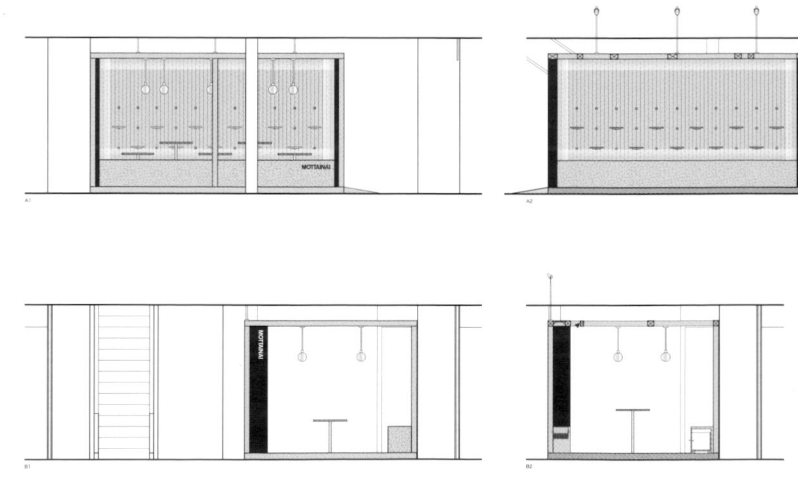
MOTTAINAI
A1
A2
MOTTAINAI
B1
B2

Display-wall systems create an aura of adventure

NIGHT

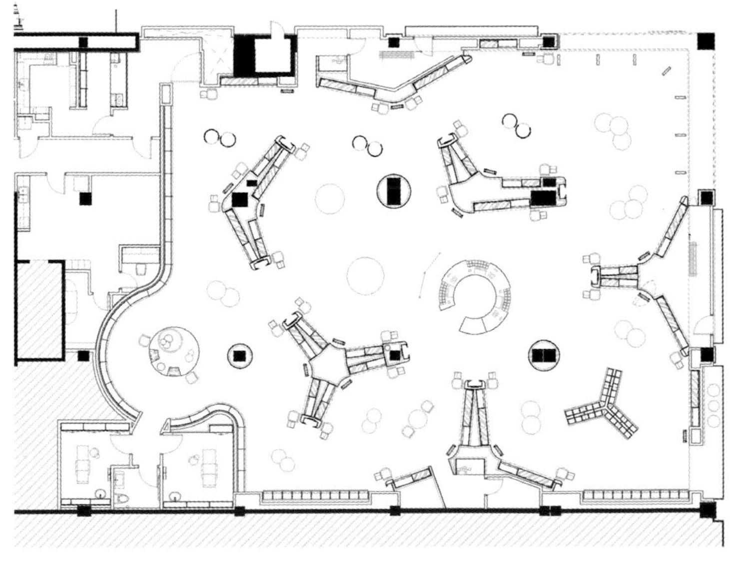

DARPHIN
PARIS

L'ORÉAL
PARIS

NAU retail locations are a **three-dimensional** realization of the company's **primary sales channel** – the Internet

nau

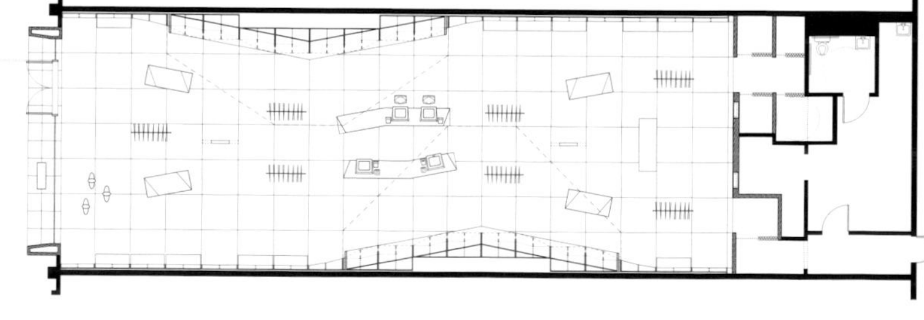

nau

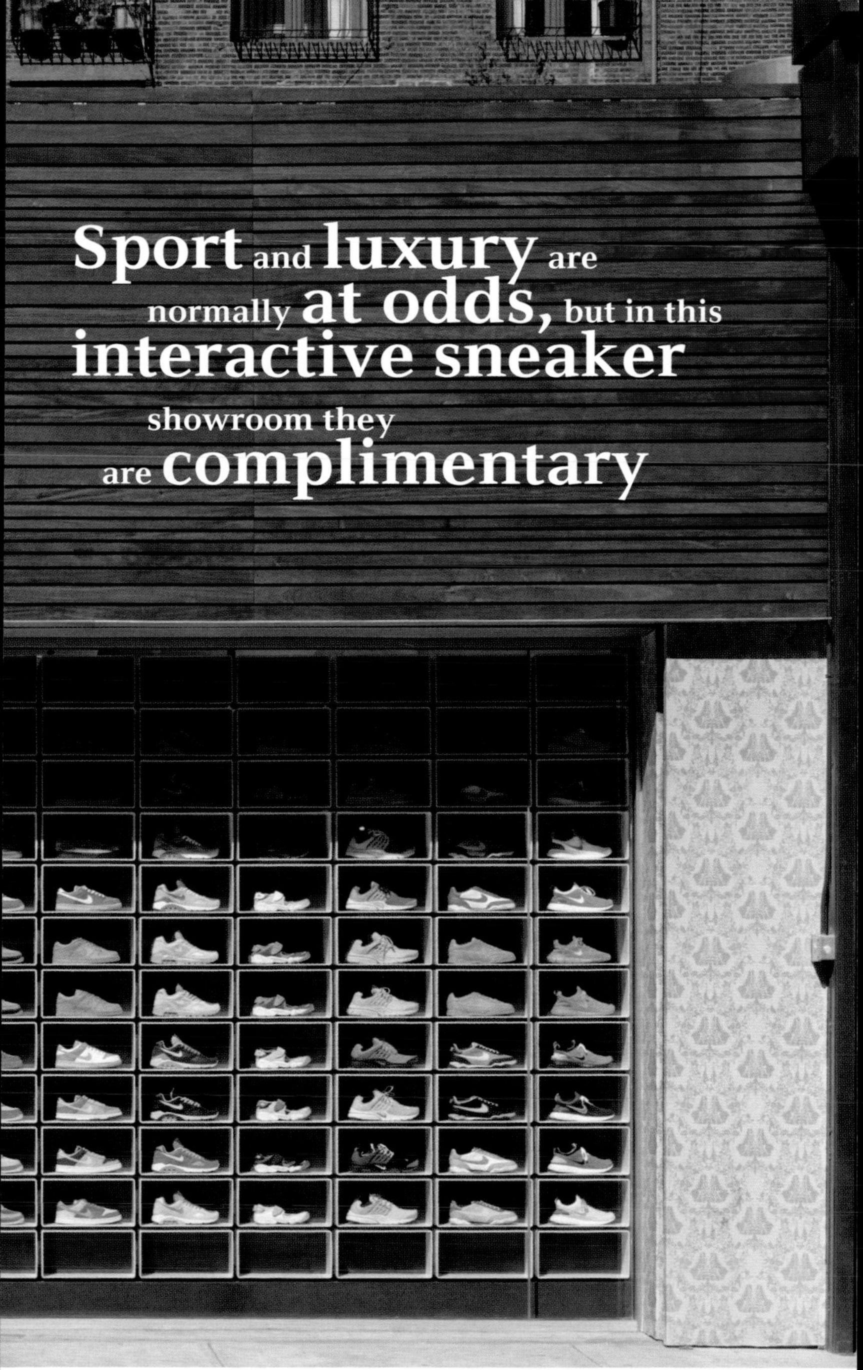

Sport and luxury are normally at odds, but in this interactive sneaker showroom they are complimentary

WAFFLE RACER II
AIR 180

The lighting resembles that of a theater stage with dramatic and varied lighting

NK HERRSKOR

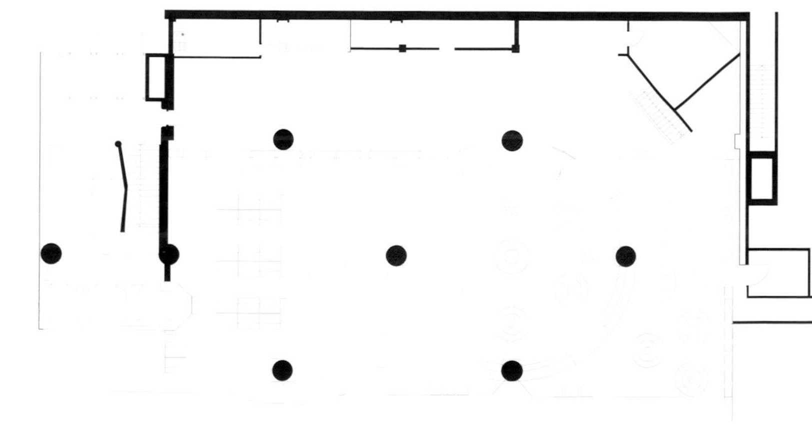

NK HERRSKOR

akki

An **artful combination** of design, **sculpture** and function create an **elegant minimalist** aesthetic in **Vancouver's** Gastown

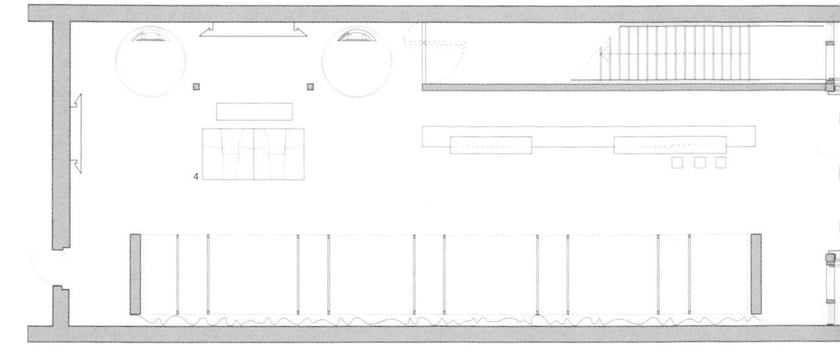
4

obakki

obakki

THE OLD SPAGHETTI FACTORY

This is a **'laboratory'** of **new products** where visitors **feel close** to the innovative **technologies** on display

monės pramogauja
Žmonės mato
Žaidimai
Mobili TV

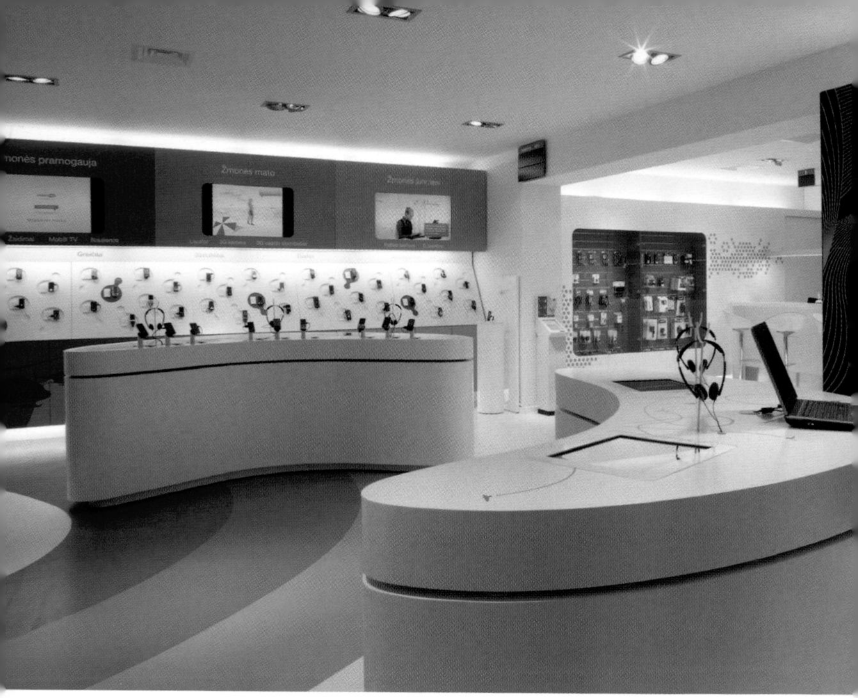

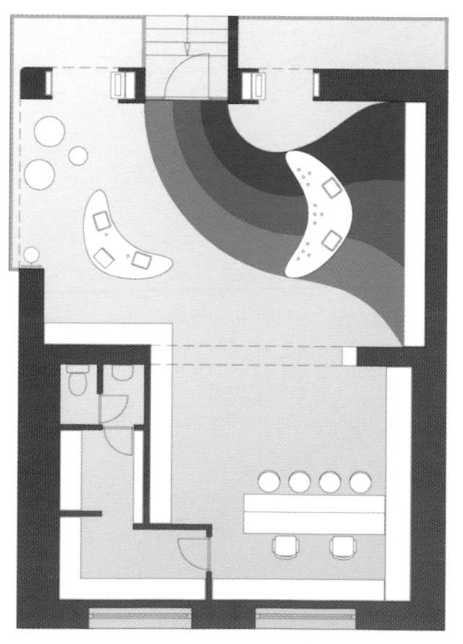

Locator
3G kamera
3G vaizdo skambučiai
Saviraiškai
Darbui

Verslui
Žmonės renkasi

Žmonės renkasi
OMNITEL

Verslui
Kasdienai
Pramogai

High-quality retail store with exclusive design

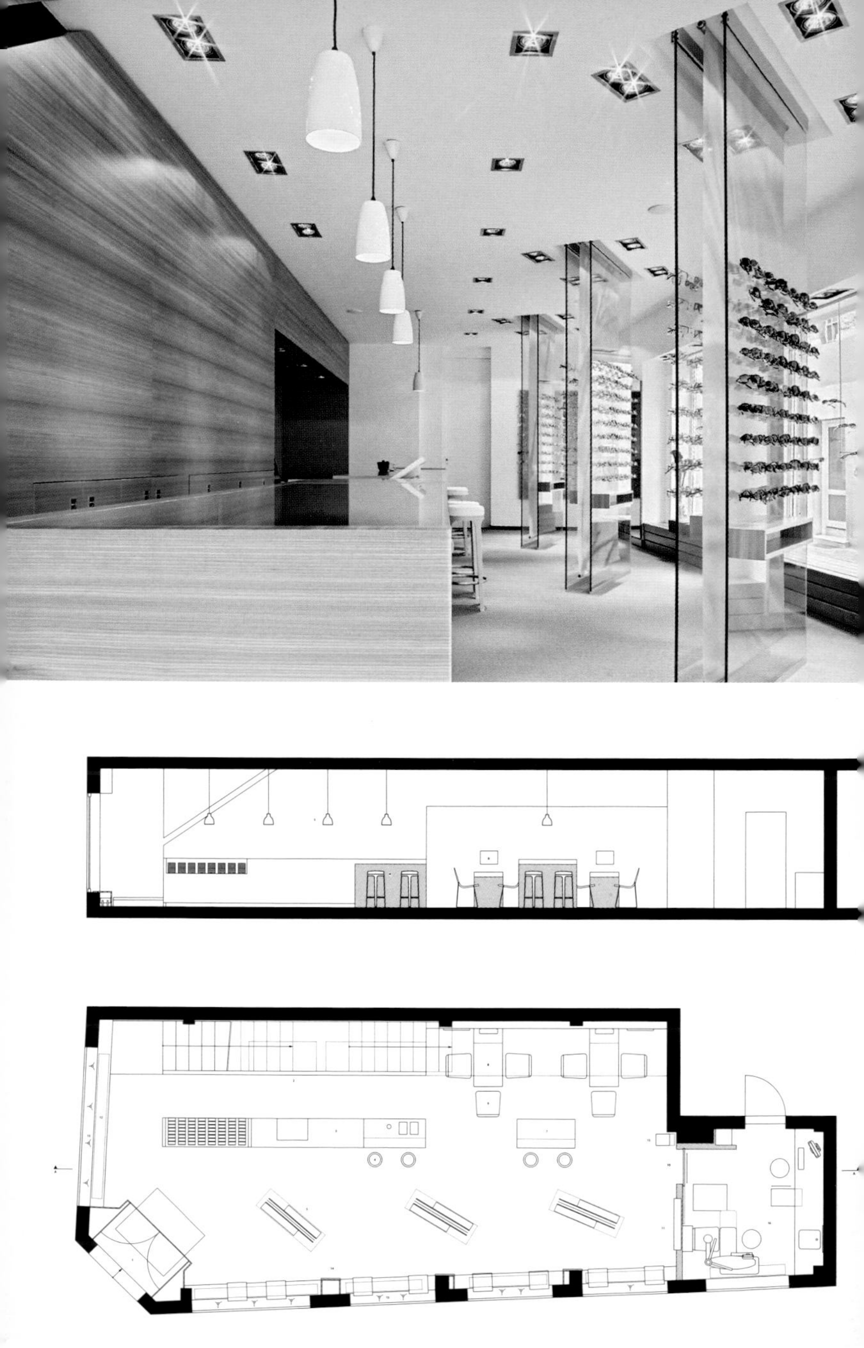

A multifunctional retail, commercial and communication space

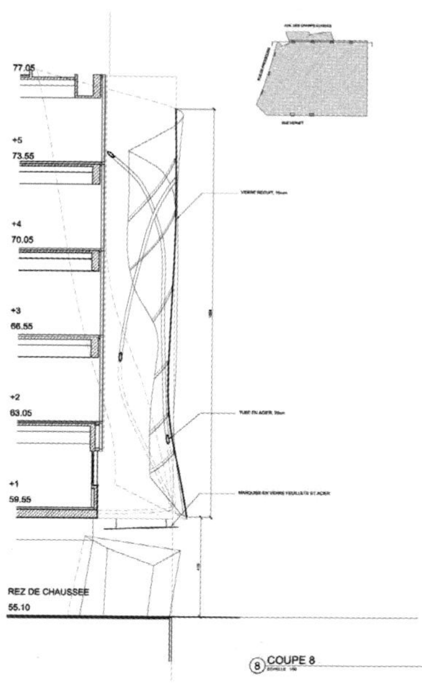
77.05
+5
73.55
+4
70.05
+3
66.55
+2
63.05
+1
59.55
REZ DE CHAUSSEE
55.10
8
COUPE 8

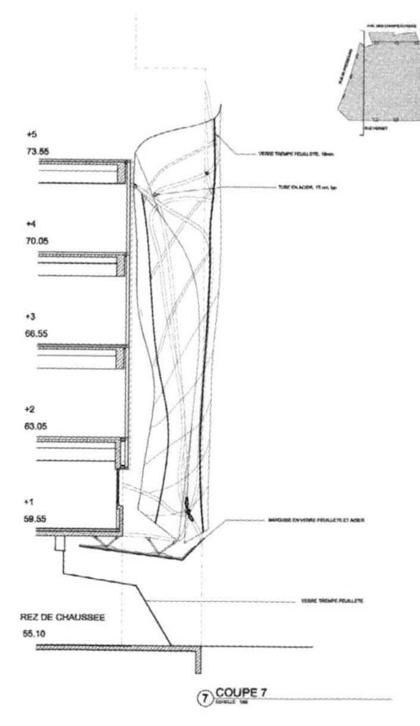
+5
73.55
+4
70.05
+3
66.55
+2
63.05
+1
59.55
MARQUISE EN VERRE FEUILLETE ET ACIER
VERRE TREMPE FEUILLETE
REZ DE CHAUSSEE
55.10
7
COUPE 7

An intentionally **pared-down palette** of materials creates a **dynamic** and **exciting space**

21
29

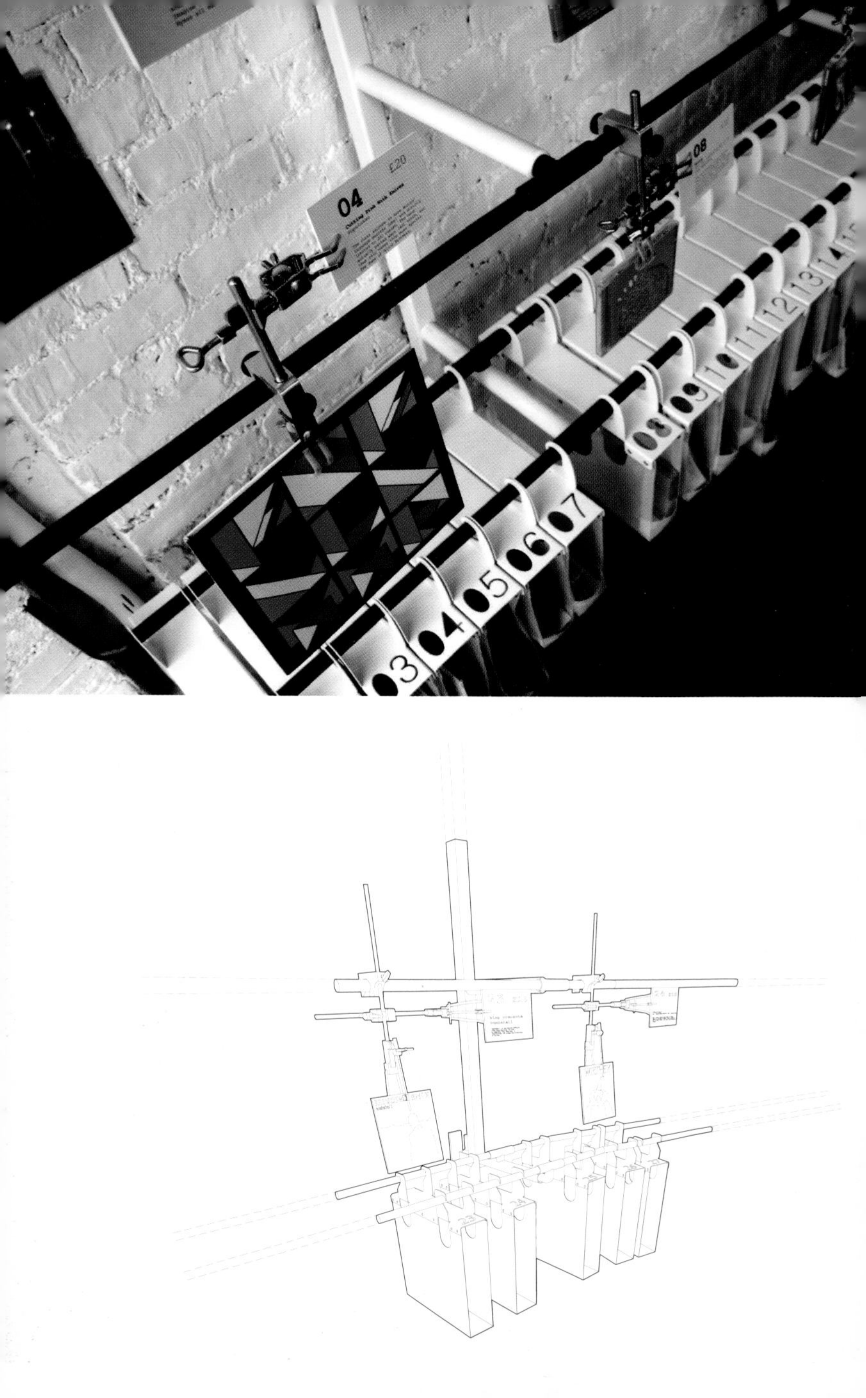

97
98
99
00
NO SLEEP TILL
BROOKLYN

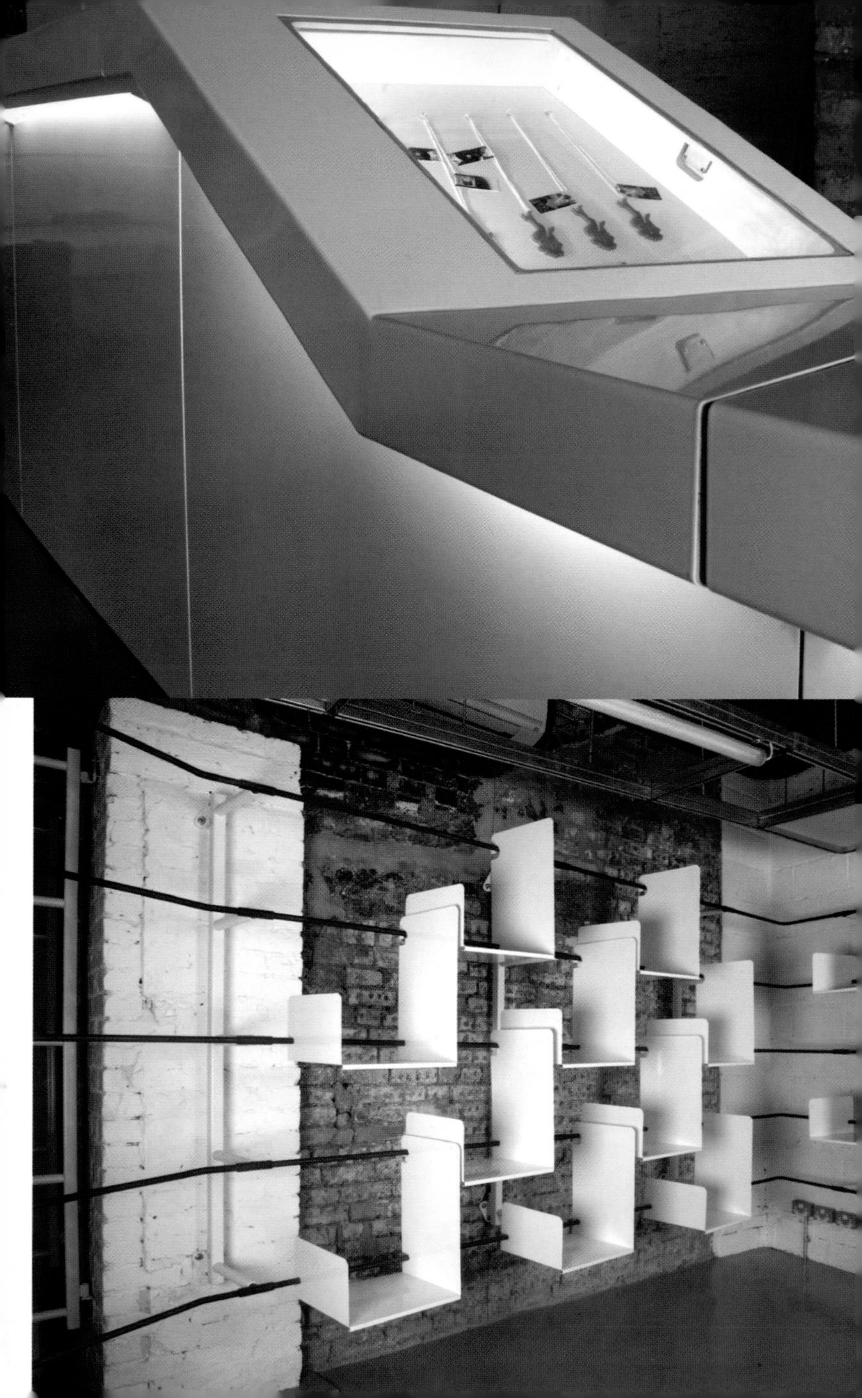

09
10
14
15
11
16
12
17
18
22
19
23
20
24
COLLAPSING CITIES
HEALTH
A
HEAVEN
GIRL ATTORNEY
TRICERATOPS
CRIMEWAVE
COURTSHIP
ZOOTHORNS
B
TABLOID SORES
GUTTER PILLS
PERFECT SKIN
LOST TIME
ADAM KESHER
Happy Vandals?
ON THE BEAT

85
93
86
90
94
95
91
LOCKED ON
92
96

98
99
00
PETE
PIRATES

The **design plays** with a sense of **depth** and **perspective,** and tricks the **eye by** extending three dimensional **shapes**

SQUEEZING
CAN PROTECT

THE
pump
TM
TONGUE
ANKLES

 Reed Space | Tokyo | upsetters architects

This space plays with ambiguous aesthetic boundaries between interior and exterior, shop and gallery

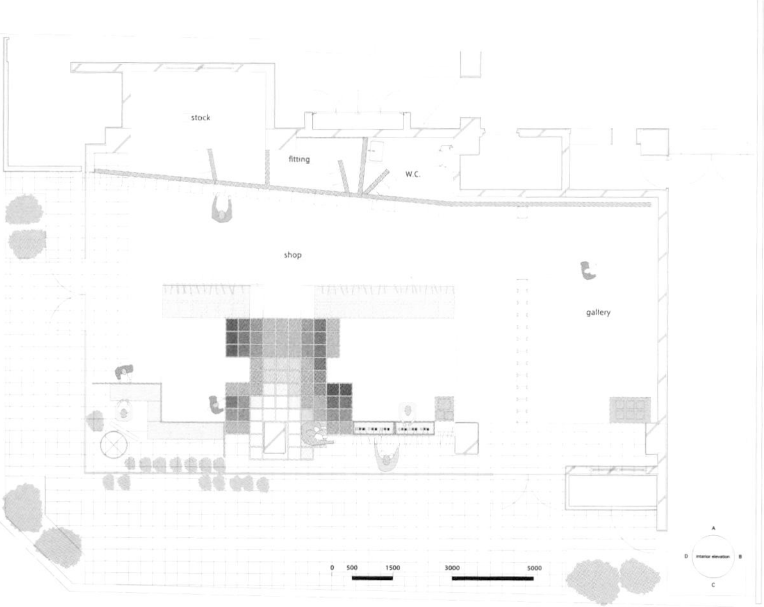

stock

fitting

W.C.

shop

gallery

0 500 1500 3000 5000

A

D interior elevation B

C

1

reed space

MIGHTY

AUG
UST
20
06
EVIL
HONEY
AUG
UST
20
06
sport
for
all
LEB
NO

This store, with its columns, steel girders and wooden floor, resembles a lounge ...

OBEY

The **net changes** its shape into partition, **counter**, **chair**, furniture and railing

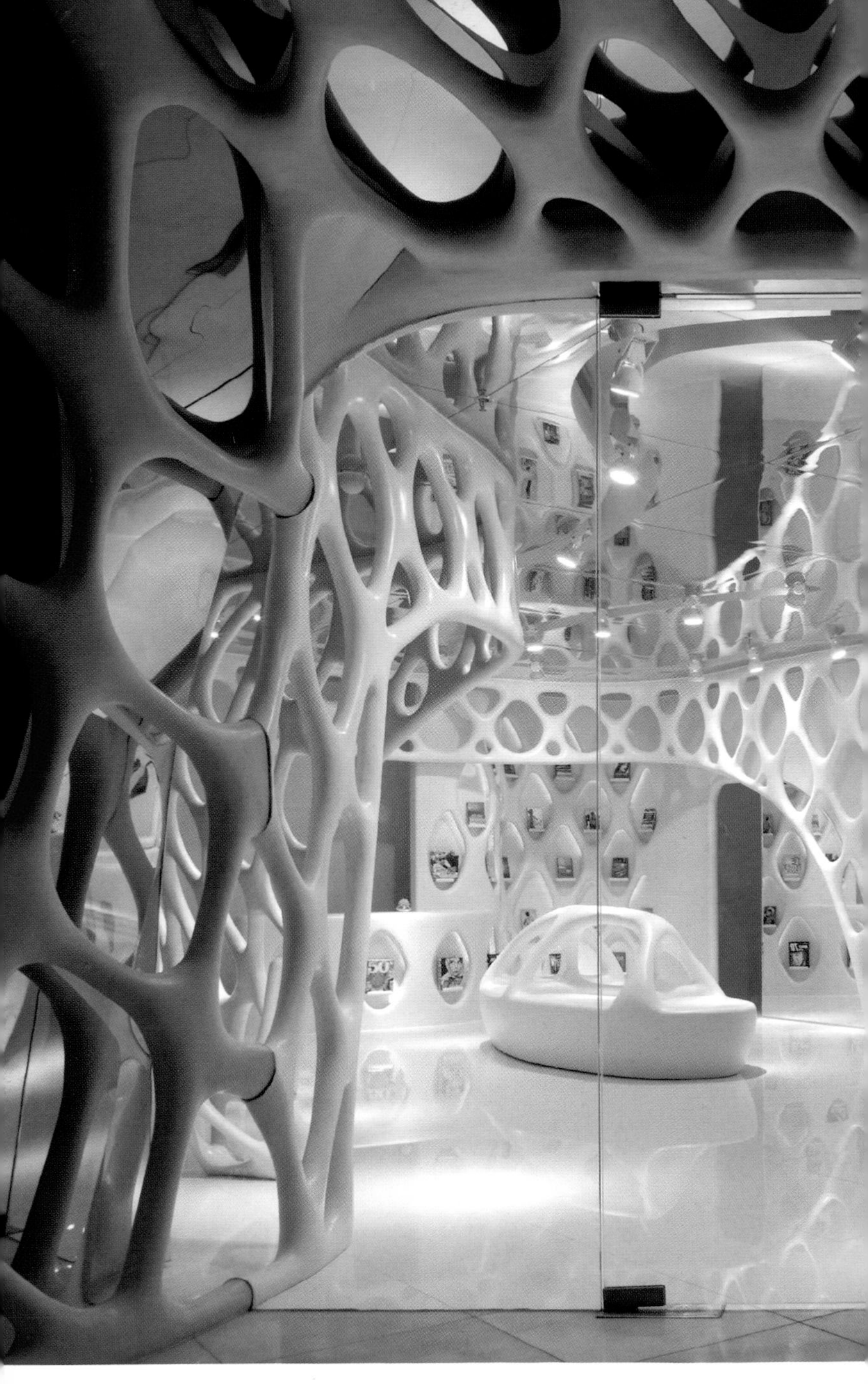

fitting room
fitting room
fitting room
fitting room
cafe
sofa
DN
DN
UP

UP
UP
UP
CASHIER

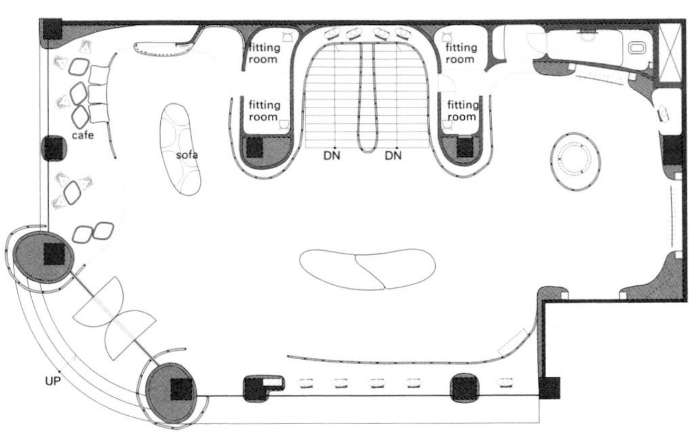

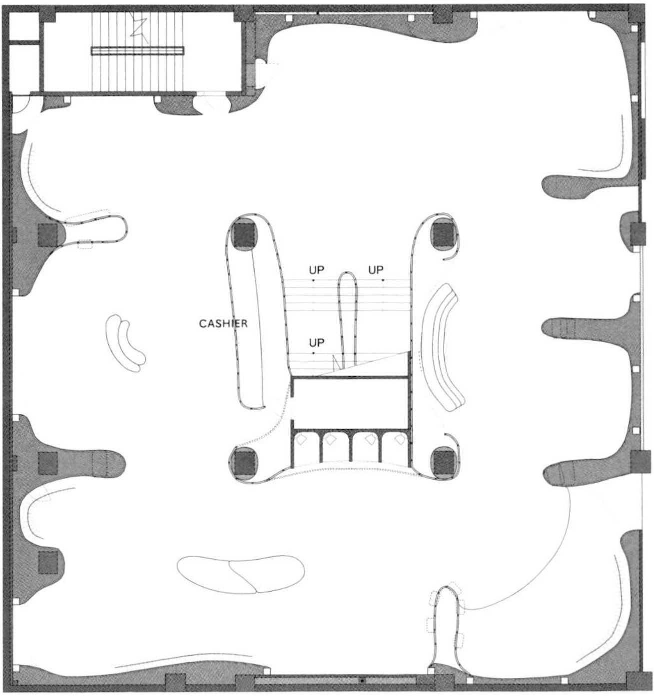

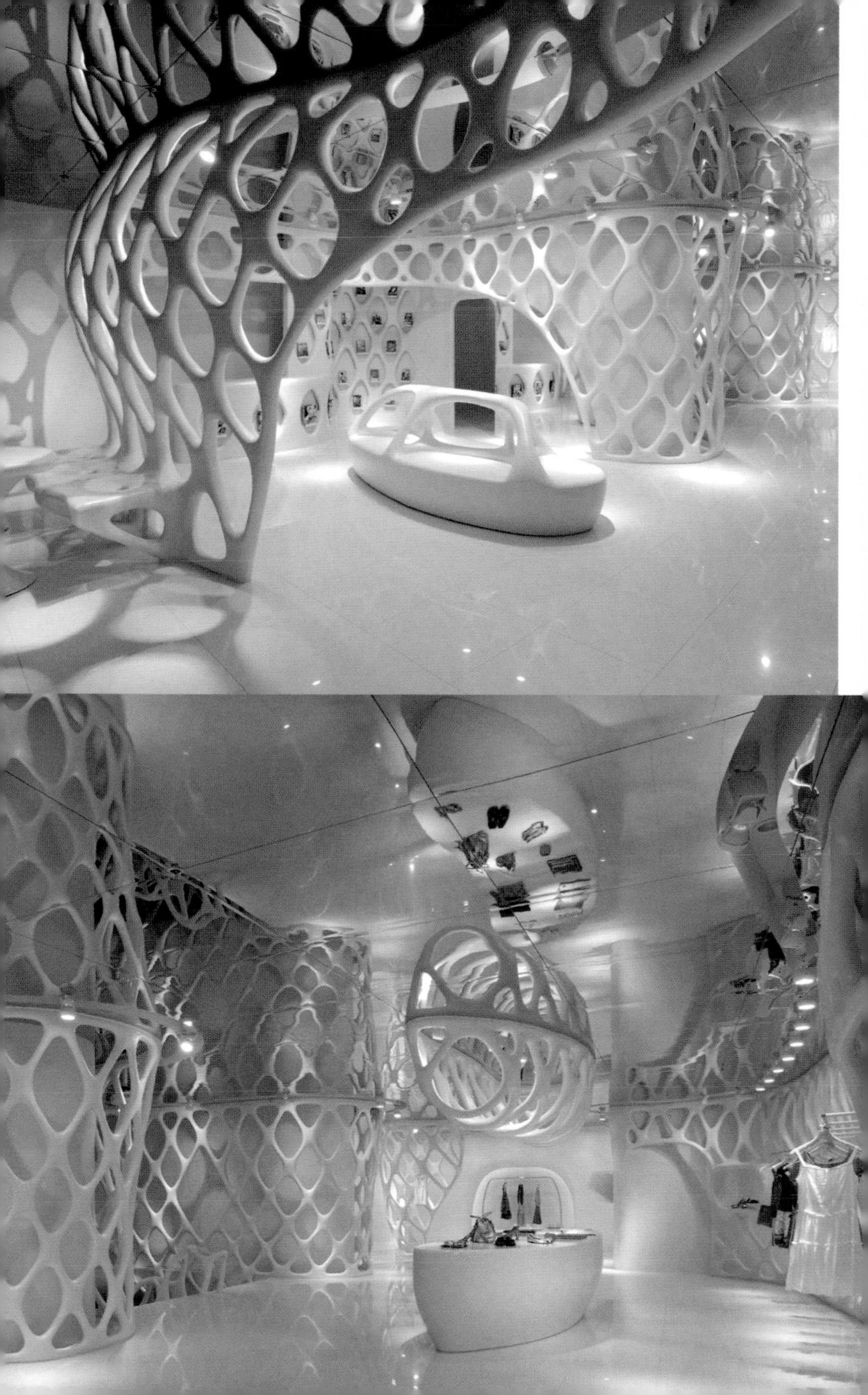

The interior **emphasizes** the rugged, **urban** and **design-oriented** style of the **company**

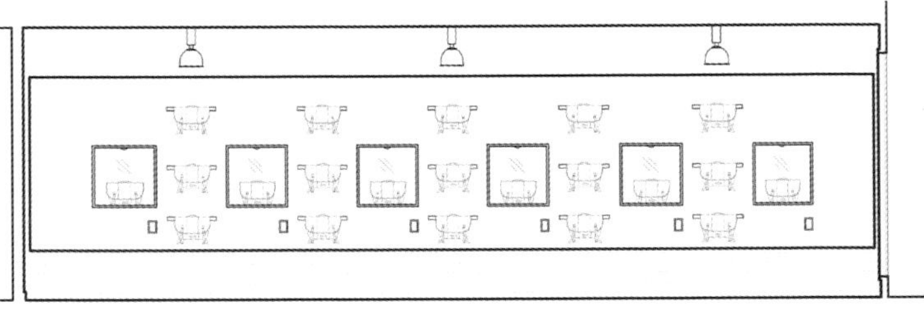

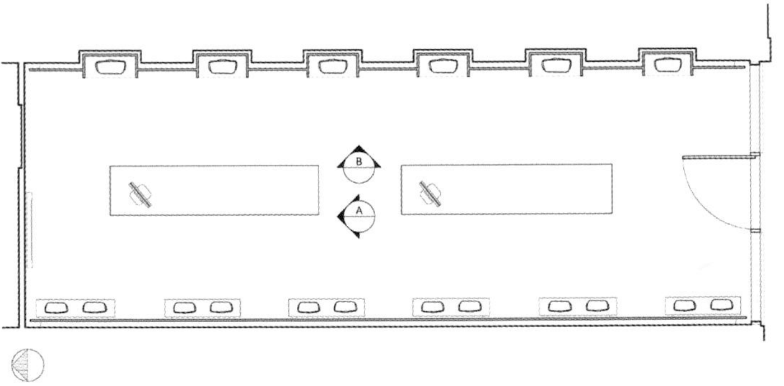
B
A

TIMBUK2
506
TIMBUK2

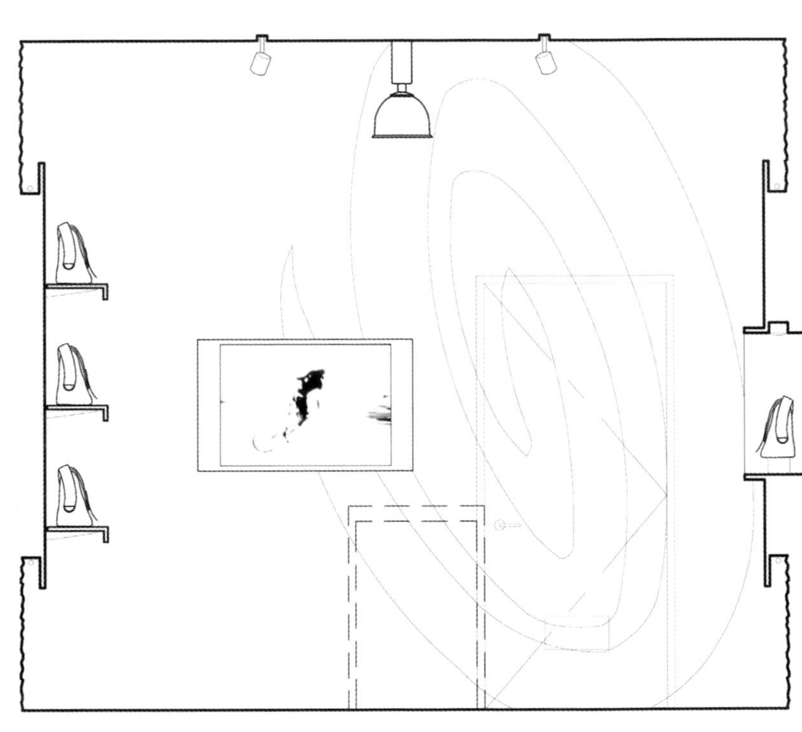

TIMBUK2

A combination of warehouse and home aesthetics

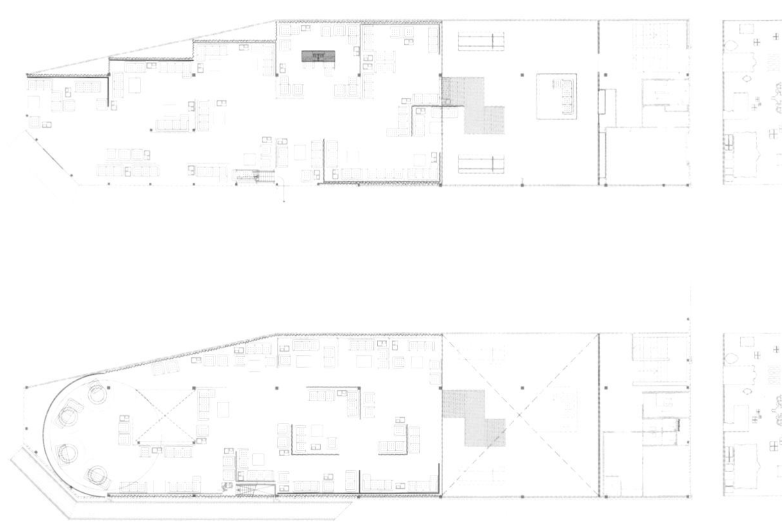

Glass veils frame the objects in a **blurred, soft geometry**

INTAGE STAR

Jessica Simpson

Jessica Simpson

An **illuminated gap** highlights the **gadgets** on display, **drawing** customers deep into the **interior**

mobilejoker.de

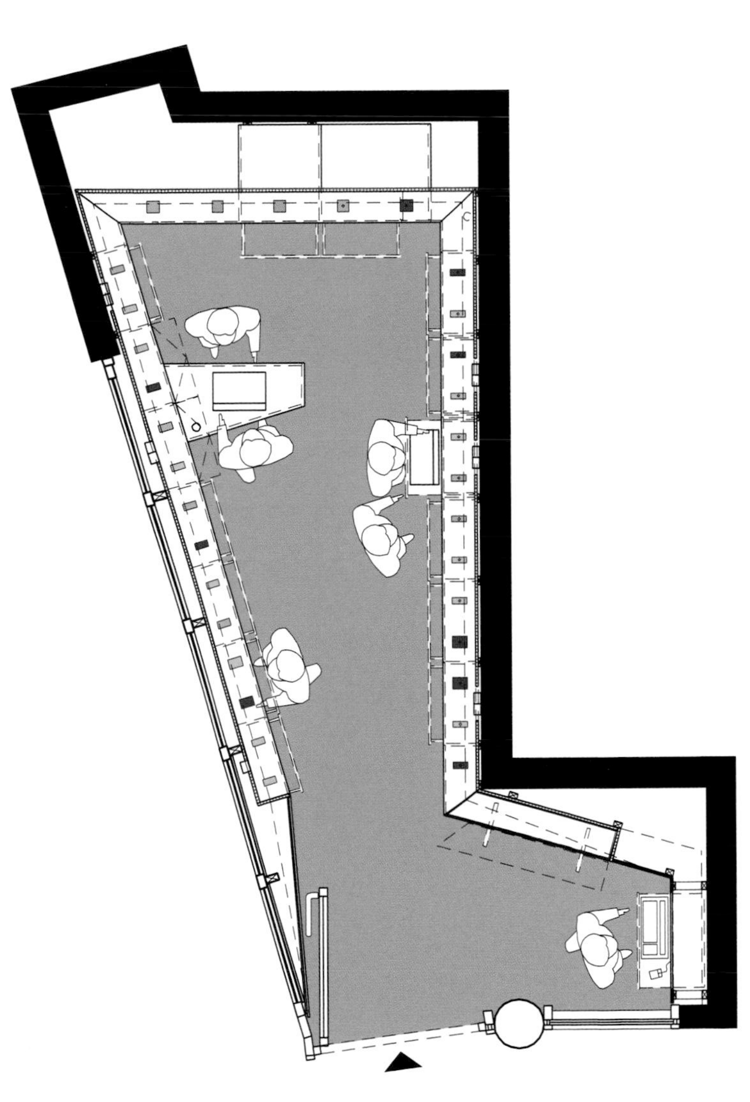

Architects Index

Picture Credits

autoban, Istanbul 198-205
Boeggly, Luc 230-231, 235a.
Tom Bonner Photography 218-225
BUILDING INC. / Michele Saee Studio 312-317
Chan, Benny, Los Angeles 54-63
Cohrssen, Jimmy 35-45
©www.cridlandphoto.com 266-273
dialogue38/toronto 140-147
Heissner, Oliver 168-173
Hitters, Juan 84-91
Hosea, Charles, London 318-325
Jil Sander: Jil Sander Crosby, New York 182-189
Kim, Yong-Kwan 64-73
Kivort / N, Jody 12-19
Kleiner, Thomas / GfG, Bremen 304-311
Kleinman, Jordan 326-335
Klomfar, Bruno, Vienna 20-27
Koji Fujii / Nacása & Partners Inc. 352-345
Kunze, Martin 394-397
Meyer, Constantin, Cologne 158-167
Morgan, Scott, Vancouver, Canada 288-295
Müller, Stefan, Berlin 28-35
Ota, Takumi 190-197
PE, Helene 282-287
Peterson, JD 346-373
Ben Rahn/A-Frame Inc. 128-139, 258-265
Ruschendorf, Grischa 118-123
Sato, Shinichi (satoshinichi.com) 252-257
Savorelli, Pietro, Florence 236-243
Schaulin, Christian 168-173
Schmitz, Arjen 206-217
Spoering, Uwe, Cologne 46-53
Staudenmaier, Eri , Los Angeles 244-251
Sternberg von, Morley 148-157
Takayama, Kozo 92-97
Tjepkema, Frank 374-383
Wakabayashi, Yusuke, Japan 336-345
Warchol, Paul, New York 174-181, 274-281,
Zupan, Bogdan 226-229

Cover: Karim Rashid Inc.